GO ahead GIRL

GO ahead GIRL

A No-Nonsense Guide To Building The Life YOU Want

Charity Carmody, LP.D.

Go Ahead Girl: A No-Nonsense Guide To Building The Life YOU Want
© Copyright 2024 Second Story Publishing

All rights reserved. No part of this publication may be reproduced, distributed or transmitted in any form or by any means, including photocopying, recording, or other electronic or mechanical methods, without the prior written permission of the publisher, except in the case of brief quotations embodied in critical reviews and certain other noncommercial uses permitted by copyright law.

Although the author and publisher have made every effort to ensure that the information in this book was correct at press time, the author and publisher do not assume and hereby disclaim any liability to any party for any loss, damage, or disruption caused by errors or omissions, whether such errors or omissions result from negligence, accident, or any other cause.

Adherence to all applicable laws and regulations, including international, federal, state and local governing professional licensing, business practices, advertising, and all other aspects of doing business in the US, Canada or any other jurisdiction is the sole responsibility of the reader and consumer.

Neither the author nor the publisher assumes any responsibility or liability whatsoever on behalf of the consumer or reader of this material. Any perceived slight of any individual or organization is purely unintentional.

The resources in this book are provided for informational purposes only and should not be used to replace the specialized training and professional judgment of a health care or mental health care professional.

Neither the author nor the publisher can be held responsible for the use of the information provided within this book. Please always consult a trained professional before making any decision regarding treatment of yourself or others.

For more information, email info@goaheadgirl.org.

ISBN: 979-8-9902353-2-8 (print hardcover)
ISBN: 979-8-9902353-3-5 (print paperback)
ISBN: 979-8-9902353-4-2 (ebook)
ISBN: 979-8-9902353-5-9 (audiobook)

Go Ahead, Girl, Join the Community!

Want to connect with other women who are building the life of their dreams?

Go to www.goaheadgirl.org

- Newsletters
- Videos
- Toolkits
- Shop
- Go Ahead Girl Groups

This book is dedicated to my incredible daughters and granddaughters: Olivia, Kristal, Vanessa, Hannah, Emery, and Iris. May you always live the life you want.

Contents

Introduction xi

Part 1 - Getting Unstuck 1
Chapter 1: Take What You Need and Leave the Rest 3
Chapter 2: Fooling Ourselves 25
Chapter 3: You Can Only Own What's Yours 54
Chapter 4: Martyrdom 72
Chapter 5: Are You Listening to Yourself? 80

Part 2 - Taking Control 97
Chapter 6: The Badass You 99
Chapter 7: The Decisive You 110
Chapter 8: The Likable You 136
Chapter 9: The Loveable You 147
Chapter 10: The Empowering You 163
Chapter 11: The Purposeful You 181
Chapter 12: The Legendary You 195

About the Author 209
References 211

Introduction

As women, we typically spend our lives devoted to the well-being of others. For many of us, this means our desires and aspirations take a back seat. That is until one of two things happens. We find ourselves headed down a road we don't want to be on or we realize we are alone in the car. Both scenarios can potentially derail us in ways we didn't anticipate.

Whether it's a launch into a new season or a transition out of a current role, at some point, everyone experiences an identity cliff. It's that moment you find yourself standing on the edge of change, questioning who you are and what you want to be.

You want to recreate yourself, but don't know how. You have responsibilities and feel like you're drowning under the weight of them, or you're experiencing new freedom but have no idea what to do with it. The change coming your way is inevitable. It may be wanted, it may be needed, or it may be forced. No matter how change is coming, you sense it.

Now is your time. You get to create your future.

This book is your no-nonsense guide to building the life YOU want. It's designed to empower women who have been living for everyone else to get honest about what they want for themselves. This book will help you understand why you do what you do and give you the tools you need to build the life YOU want.

The book is divided into two parts: getting unstuck and taking control.

Part one provides the tools you need to deconstruct inherited ideologies and thought patterns that are no longer useful. You will identify the areas you can and can't control and uncover ways you've fooled yourself. You will learn how to change the way you think and talk.

Part two is all about taking control of your future. Each chapter in this section identifies elements of the future you. These chapters will provide you with insights on how to present yourself to the world, make decisions, improve relationships, find purpose, and create a legacy to be proud of.

The end of each chapter has a Building Blocks section that is a summary of key take-aways. I've also included Toolkits that you can use for your individual self-work or group discussions.

This book is not a comprehensive to-do list for every area of your life. It's a collection of the major life lessons I have learned as a boss, mentor, professor, consultant, partner, mother, creator, and friend. I've been married for thirty years, have close relationships with my four children and grandchildren, built several very successful businesses and nonprofits, and have mentored and taught hundreds of women.

You will read stories about my mistakes and what I've learned from them. Although our experiences aren't the same, you're going to resonate with the struggles and victories we experience as women. This is your life. You're the one who gets to live it. Build it the way you want to experience it.

PART 1
Getting Unstuck

Chapter 1

Take What You Need and Leave the Rest

There was no plan to dismantle my life; it just kind of happened. By every standard, my 2018 self was crushing the game. I'd been happily married to Kris for twenty-four years, had four grown children doing well, two beautiful grandchildren, owned a successful insurance company, was co-pastoring a large church, and won awards for my non-profit work. In my mind, the equation was working. You know, the equation:

Work hard + take care of everyone else + stay in your lane = a good woman's life

Life isn't a big math equation, however, and doing what you should doesn't necessarily give you the life YOU want, just the life EVERYONE ELSE wants.

We've been told what to think our whole lives. We want to think of ourselves as self-actualized and independent, but how we think and what we believe are the results of the ideas we have been taught. Each bit of information we take in is confirmed or rejected by our own experience. When we face a new situation and can't draw from our own lived experiences, we rely on the experiences of someone we trust.

As children, we don't get to choose the information given to us. It just goes down the hatch, like it or not. Family and culture quickly inform us about "people like us." Each social group has its beliefs and behaviors. Even when things appear unstructured or haphazard, it only means that chaos and dysfunction are the existing norms.

We aren't difficult creatures to understand. We do what we've been told works, or what we have found works for us, and we will keep doing the same thing until we come to a new understanding that requires change.

Great Awakenings

To say I was sheltered is an understatement. My family was loving, working class, and lived in a safe neighborhood. My childhood revolved around school, work, friends, sports, church, and community service. Understandably, my friends all thought like I did because we all drank the same Kool-Aid. As an adult, my beliefs hadn't changed much from childhood. I didn't have a real understanding of opinions contradicting mine because everyone I respected and the information I consumed confirmed what I was told.

I grew up in a family of pastors, and being raised in church leadership meant I started teaching Sunday school and leading at a very young age. I never wanted to be a pastor; it just kind of happened. In reality, I had always been one. It was the only life I knew.

Growing up in the church exposed me to both the light and shadow sides of humans. People say that the church is full of hypocrites, and they are right. Even with the best intentions and efforts, hypocrisy is an unavoidable byproduct of a society that expects perfection. Churches attract people who want to feel 'right' while fighting their urges to do 'wrong.' It's a tough battle.

Naively, I thought my family was nearly perfect and didn't have a bunch of secrets, but in 2018, I found out that I was wrong. For some people, finding out a loved one had a secret life may be understood or even expected. Looking back, they could find clues of the person being unhappy or hiding secrets. Not me, I was completely blindsided. My family had always been such a pillar of ideal Christianity, at home and in the community, so it knocked me off kilter.

Do you know that feeling when you find out someone has lied to you? At first, you can't believe it. Then the shit hits the fan and you're confronted with undeniable proof. It makes you reel back and take inventory of everything they've ever said, and now things hit differently. That's what happened to me.

Maybe it was my deep love for justice or my rigid rule-following personality, but I couldn't stand the feeling of being duped. In my anger and disbelief, I began digging into my upbringing and started asking hard questions about the ideologies that had formed my mindset.

This wasn't about any one person's actions. I've had enough life experience and education to understand the complexities of why we do the things we do. I began the upheaval *because* I understood that behind every action is a cause, and every good lesson was created with an agenda in mind.

To be honest, some things had been bothering me about my religion for a long time. Is it odd that I never asked why a good God would create people inherently bad? Or how did Moses write about what happened in the Garden of Eden when Adam and Eve were the only ones there? Did God need the Christian crusaders to defend his name by killing over a million people? Did Samson really lose his muscle power because his hair got cut off? Isn't the whole Bible written by a bunch of men writing about one big, powerful man? These silly questions led me to more substantial ones. I hadn't felt free to question things until I was in my forties.

I couldn't avoid the issues that were haunting me about my faith because every day of every week, I was responsible for representing and teaching the very beliefs I was questioning. It was the perfect storm. My world-shattering provided a beautiful separation of personhood that demanded thoughtful reconstruction. Now was the time to give my muffled mumblings the air they needed to breathe.

Curiosity is a beautiful thing. It's what drives growth, innovation, and science. The approach of living by faith without questioning inconsistencies was coming head-to-head with my curiosity. My long-standing, nagging questions started to come out. Once out of the bag, my skepticism ran deep. I had always considered myself a lover of the truth, but was I? To be a lover of the truth, one must be committed to questioning and experimentation. **You can't be a truth seeker if you feel you already have the answers.**

Looking for Proof

I've been a financial advisor and business owner for over 20 years. My professional life was driven by sound evidence-based principles that required and tracked proof. My internal eyes roll when people assume that the mathematics of time, compounding, and economics don't apply to them, that they were somehow going to beat all of history and math with their self-discovered strategy.

I also own an insurance company. Selling insurance showed me very quickly how much we all lie to ourselves. It's surprising when some clients act like they and their families are never going to experience death, tragedy, or loss, even though all evidence points to that certainty. I can't tell you how often I've heard people say they won't get into an accident because they are "good drivers," as if they were the only ones on the road and can control how other people drive. Stupid rationale, much?

I saw inconsistencies in others, but didn't in my own life. Until I did. Then I had to ask myself, "Am I willing to put everything about my life on the table for true evaluation? My relationships, my parenting, my beliefs, all of it. Am I willing to re-think it all with an open mind and heart? How about I keep what is working and leave the rest?" It turns out that the simple scientific method of questioning, testing, and proving was exactly where I needed to begin.

Science differs from other subjects like history, language, and religion. Becoming a scientist for my own life has been one of the most freeing disciplines. Instead of teaching myself to adhere to existing precepts, it's taught me to question prior understanding. It permitted me to separate my opinions and beliefs from my personhood. When we women view our opinions and beliefs as their own entity, we get to test them on their own merits. Science is looking for progress instead of preservation. I want to be a person of progress. Reading this book is proof that you do, too.

What you are looking for as an observer of your own life is proof, what your life has shown you. It is not what someone has told you about your life, but what you have observed and experienced about yourself. When we get truly curious about our lives, we prove we are willing to learn and change.

Changing your mind isn't a flaw. It's a strength. It means with your learning; you dare to be corrected. In Adam Grant's book *Think Again*, he explains that changing your mind because you've encountered stronger evidence or logic isn't being flighty; it's a sign that you are learning. Being a person who is willing to learn and grow should always be applauded.

Self–correcting isn't for the faint of heart, though. We take on the risk of alienation and rejection when we go through the change process, but what we gain is the life we want. Not the life that someone else says we should have but the life we truly deserve.

The long-held beliefs and strategies you are struggling with may be different from mine. But trust me, I understand your struggle and would love for you to re-evaluate your beliefs. This reckoning process is about *your* life and freedom, not someone else's. Each of us is a product of all the ideologies we were taught, and comparing ourselves will lead us down a trap that produces dependents and victims.

We all have different starting lines, but our potential for winning is unlimited. It's time to have a life that is consistent with who you want to be, how you want to think, where you want to go, and who you want to love. A life you can be proud of.

Imagining a Different Future

I know you've had those great awakening moments. Those times when you were confronted with a new reality that didn't fit with what you knew of the world. These moments don't have to be catastrophic. Maybe they come because we learned something new or experienced a different perspective. For many of us in America, the events surrounding the murder of George Floyd sparked in us an awareness of systemic racism that we had not yet understood. For others, a great awakening comes when we gain or lose a friend or partner. Sometimes, it's a culmination of new realities that cause a tipping point. These new realities give us the space to imagine our future differently.

Imagine yourself in one of these moments. You have been given new information that could have a significant impact on the way you live and how you think. Maybe you are in one right now. What are you going to do with this new information? The way I see it, you have two options: you can tunnel, or you can tower.

Think of what a *tunnel* is. It's an alternate pathway that often runs parallel to the pathway above ground. It is confined and isolated. Light has to be manufactured. It may feel safe to be insulated from the world above, but it also means that you don't see the sun or experience adventure. When we tunnel, we get so caught up in our perspective and desire that we don't realize we have curated an environment that doesn't support growth. We isolate ourselves this way. The only people in the tunnel with us are those who are willing to live in the same alternate reality.

We tunnel when we refuse to acknowledge and accept new information that contradicts what we have known. It is the proverbial "bury your head in the sand" approach. Sometimes, we just don't have the heart or capacity to accept what it is at that moment. We feel there is too much at stake. We put the new information through a filter of our liking so that we can understand it better. We come up with a reason why it can't be true. We file the edges down so that the puzzle piece still fits.

We blame ourselves, someone else, or some external force, anything to make sense of the inconsistency. Unfortunately, tunneling only leads to dark and isolated places. When we choose to tunnel, we get stuck digging and digging. We have to rationalize what we've already rationalized from what we rationalized before. It goes on and on. We excuse bad behavior in ourselves and others. The further down the tunnel, the longer and more treacherous the journey to the light.

You know you've started to tunnel when you refuse external input that is different from your own, isolate yourself, feel like everyone is out to get you, or are spiraling into a destructive narrative about your situation. Thinking too much about our feelings, emotions, and desires can quickly become tunneling behavior. In doing this, we lose the perspective needed to be healthy and happy.

When a group of people tunnel together, they fortify each other's unhealthy barriers. This groupthink can lead to abuse and cultish behavior. A friend of ours tells a story of living in an underground bunker for over a month because he was in a cult that thought the world was coming to an end. You can tunnel both mentally and physically. This is real, y'all.

Your other option, when confronted with new information, is to *tower*. Instead of digging down, you climb, and you climb high enough to examine your life from an elevated place. You distance yourself enough mentally and emotionally to view your choices and circumstances. It helps you see the bigger picture. **Towering means that you step back and get curious.**

You climb up in that tower and look down at the situation and your life. What journey brought you here to this impasse? When you look at your path ahead, where does it lead? Do your best in this moment to remove the ego, shame, and emotion. Just observe your path and what got you here. What were you taught? What information did you consume on your own accord? Who is on the path with you? Who isn't? What signs did you follow? Which ones did you miss? Would you have taken a different path if you had it to do over? There is no shame here. You are a curious observer. What do you see?

Towering is the opposite of naval gazing. Instead of focusing on your own emotions and feelings, look at them like you are someone else. What would you think of your choices if you were an external observer? Would they be logical and rational? Were your choices based on emotion? If you were someone else, would you understand why you chose the traveling partners you did? What did they bring on the journey?

We tend to remember the past in broad strokes. When I tower and let myself get curious, it is helpful to write down and rehearse why I did what I did in the order of my decisions. In times of questioning, major life choices we've made can be confused or skewed.

Many years ago, my husband chose to shut down his contracting company. When he is feeling down, he questions his decision and wonders if it was a mistake. He can get stuck in that regret until he decides to tower and reminds himself of all the reasons he made that decision. He made the best decision with the information he had at the time and in the face of many obstacles that had presented themselves. Often, we have made the right decision, but we get stuck in thoughts of regret when we fail to tower and remember what the path was actually like when we made those choices.

There are times when getting curious and towering will lead us to the determination that we did the right thing, and other times we realize we made the wrong call. That's ok. We now have information we didn't have before. When we understand and can articulate why we did what we did, we can make better decisions moving forward. In the famous words of Mya Angelou "I did then what I knew how to do. Now that I know better, I do better."

Your Possibility Pictures

When studying our lives, we need to understand that everything we do and say is driven by what we think is or isn't possible for us in the future. I call these visions of our future, possibility pictures.

Imagine that you're having a rare transparent moment with your best friend, parent, or partner. You've been sipping wine and chatting about everything you would want to be or accomplish in your lifetime. If they were to ask you to imagine what is possible for you in the areas of your relationships, body, work, or finances, what would you say? What do you consider to be possible for you?

When I'm trying to decide where I'll have dinner, I don't think of restaurants that aren't in my city. When women look for potential partners, they might not consider that their soulmate may reside in Belize if it's somewhere they've never been. We often don't see the many options in front of us because we simply aren't considering them as a possibility.

That said, if we can uncover our deeply held beliefs about what is possible for us, we can work backward and better understand why we have done and said the things we have. Your possibility pictures are the background of all your experiences, they color everything.

It is important to note that possibility pictures are not fairy tales. I can't be the Queen of England. I'm not British, and I wasn't born into nobility. It's not possible for me to do many things given my build, brain, situation, and relationships. But that doesn't mean there aren't a slew of things that are possible for me.

By honestly describing what we believe is possible, we uncover both our deepest desires and limiting beliefs. If you want to dig into this and find out, go through the possibility picture exercise at the end of this chapter.

Becoming a Curious Four-Year-Old

If you've been around little kids, you know that part of constructing their worldview is asking questions. Lots and lots of questions. It's "Why mommy?" over and over from the back seat of the car. This phase of child development gives us an excellent example of how we should approach our re-discovery. When a child asks why after each answer, there is no maliciousness or judgment. They are innocent. They simply want to understand. They are creating a context to make sense of why things around them occur. We should do the same.

Within the scientific process, once you've observed a phenomenon and identified what you think is occurring, you go out and gather data to either prove or disprove your assumptions. You do this all the time when you care about something or someone. It's like when you can tell your best friend is "off," and you keep asking them what's going on until they finally admit what they're upset about.

When my teenagers used to get angsty, I could tell something was wrong because they would huff under their breath or throw their hoods up and go silent. I might make assumptions about what's wrong, but I really won't know until I do some digging. Did they fight with a friend? Did someone say something rude at school? Are they mad at me? You get the idea.

If we make the mistake of tunneling as a parent, we might take one look at our angsty teen, make assumptions without seeking out the truth, or even worse, make it about ourselves (believe me, I've been there). We are unhelpful when we do this. How can we help if we don't have the facts?

It's the same thing with you. Unless you are willing to recognize your actions, you may not understand what you do, and that is the point of this process. If you want to get into the nitty gritty of your mind, work through the Toolkit at the end of the chapter.

Finding Your Enough

Four-year-olds asking why over and over are only cute for a while, then it gets annoying. Even when it's our kids asking, we sometimes get to the point of saying things like "because I said so," "because I'm the mom, " or "that's just the way it is." Likewise, you may have an enough-is-enough moment with yourself. Yes, we all want answers to questions, but you must know when to stop asking. Building the life you want requires forward momentum. And, once you've observed and understood this, you must act toward your new truth. Launching and testing your new understanding are the adventures required to build the life you want.

I've encountered so many women who are stuck in what-if questions, past regrets, and indecision, but it doesn't do anyone any good. Eventually we all just have to put one foot in front of the other.

To move forward, you've got to find your "enough." Finding your enough means you understand all you can for now, or you are fine not understanding. It's where I had to get with some of my deeper questions about my faith. I've found my enough in not having the answers to everything anymore. Releasing myself from the need to be right was the beginning of my liberation.

Ironically, I'm finding that my heart is more gracious and loving now than when it was part of a religion I followed. I let myself see strengths instead of weaknesses in myself and others. This is my enough. My enough is to accept who my partner is and will be even after thirty years of marriage. Making peace with who my children are and who I am are my enough. I am consciously eliminating the agendas, the what-ifs, and unrealistic standards.

How about you? Have you found your enough? Are you still asking yourself the same old questions that have either been answered or have no answer? Are you ready to move forward and let the answers you've found be sufficient for now?

You may not be finding your enough because you still need more information to resolve it. Identify what you need to know to get closure and move forward. This may mean having a conversation you've been avoiding, experimenting with an idea, or changing that relationship.

Whatever you need to know or do to get to your enough, weigh the consequences carefully first. If the cost to get the information you want is too high, then you don't need the answer.

For instance, you may want to know if you would have had better chemistry with your high-school lover than your partner. Is that knowledge worth blowing up your relationship? Maybe you're thinking you would like a different career more than the one you have. What's that knowledge worth to you? Is it worth starting over? It takes a long time to understand a career or truly know a person. Also, just trying something out doesn't give you the same experience as being in something for the long-haul. Be smart. There is a substantial difference between need and want.

As you'll see in Chapter 5, finding your enough is when you've closed your answer loop for a while. Finding your enough will reduce your mental load because you've done the hard work of getting curious, asking questions, and finding enough of an answer to satisfy your mind for now. You may not have all the details or know why you are where you are, but you understand enough to stop wondering why you are doing what you are doing.

When you are satisfied with your analysis, you can now act on your enough. Moving forward, you get to decide what your possibility pictures look like. You get to decide which people, systems, beliefs, limitations, and strengths are a part of them.

Like a backpacking trip, every element of your life has a mental, emotional, physical, and spiritual load. Let the questions that have been answered rest. Let the unwarranted insecurities fall away. Let the strengths you've identified remain. Take what you need for the journey ahead, and leave the rest.

Building Blocks

- We do what we've been told works, or what we have found works for us, and we will keep doing the same thing until we come to a new understanding that requires change.

- You can't be a truth seeker if you feel you already have the answers.

- Changing your mind isn't a flaw. It's a strength. It means with your learning, you dare to be corrected.

- New realities give us the space to imagine our futures differently.

- We "tunnel" when we refuse to acknowledge and accept new information that contradicts what we have known.

- We "tower" when we step back and get curious. We distance ourselves enough mentally and emotionally to view our choices and circumstances as a bigger picture.

- When we understand and can articulate why we did what we did, we can make better decisions moving forward.

- Everything we do and say is driven by what we think is or isn't possible for us in the future.
- Possibility pictures uncover both our deepest desires and limiting beliefs.
- Finding your "enough" means that you understand all that you can for now, or you are fine not understanding. Finding your "enough" is when you've closed your answer loop for now.
- Let the questions that have been answered rest. Let the unwarranted insecurities fall away. Let the strengths you've identified remain. Take what you need for the journey ahead, and leave the rest.

Chapter 1: Take What You Need and Leave the Rest

Q1. Great awakenings are moments when you begin the journey of rethinking a long-held belief or life experience. What great awakenings have you experienced, and what were your nagging questions?

_____
_____
_____
_____

Q2. Once you've claimed and voiced opinions or beliefs, it can be hard to retract them because you've made internal vows, or you fear the social ramifications. Being able to change your mind because you've been presented with better evidence means you are learning and getting wiser. Are there any opinions or beliefs you've had that you would like to be able to change but are afraid to? What do you think will happen if you change your mind? What would need to happen for you to feel good about changing your mind?

_____
_____
_____
_____

Q3. You tunnel when you refuse to acknowledge and accept new information that contradicts what you have known. Identify times when you've tunneled. In what areas are you tunneling now? Do you see any patterns in your tunneling behavior?

_____
_____
_____
_____

Q4. You tower when you step back and get curious. You distance yourself enough mentally and emotionally to view your choices and circumstances as a bigger picture. Imagine you are someone else observing your situation from afar. Write down the pivotal points along the journey that led you to where you are now. What was your rationale at that point? What does that rationale tell you about yourself?

_____
_____
_____
_____

Q5. Finding your enough means that you understand all that you can for now, or you are fine not understanding. Finding your enough is when you've closed your answer loop for now. In which areas have you found your enough?

_____
_____
_____
_____

Q6. In which areas do you need to find your enough? How will you find it?

_____
_____
_____
_____

Possibility Picture Exercise

Everything you do and say is driven by what you think is or isn't possible for you within your lifetime. To draw your possibility pictures, you'll need to ask yourself some questions about several areas of your life.

By answering these questions honestly, you uncover both your deepest desires and limiting beliefs.

What is possible for me in my romantic relationship(s)?

_____
_____
_____
_____

What is possible for me physically?

_____
_____
_____
_____

What is possible for me in my friendships?

_____
_____
_____
_____

What is possible for me financially?

_____
_____
_____
_____

What is possible for me in my work?

_____
_____
_____
_____

What is possible for me in my family?

_____
_____
_____
_____

What is possible for me in my passion projects?

_____
_____
_____
_____

What is possible for me in my leisure time?

_____
_____
_____
_____

What is possible for me in my spiritual life?

_____
_____
_____
_____

You've identified what you believe is possible for you, but there is more to it. Every possibility picture has six elements that provide context for why we have envisioned our possibilities the way we have. The elements are:

- People
- History
- Systems
- Beliefs
- Limitations
- Strengths

Let's clarify why your possibility pictures look the way they do. Take each possibility picture and drill down even further by asking yourself these things in each area:

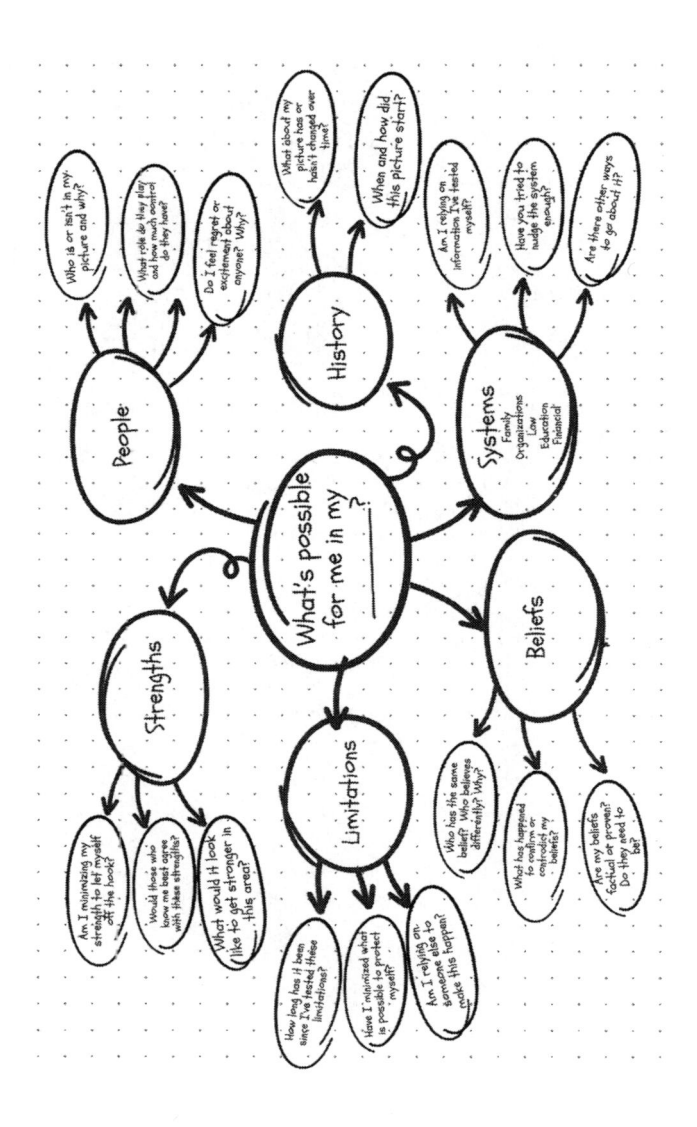

Remember not to judge yourself in this process. You are an observer of your life. What are you seeing more clearly about yourself? Let yourself learn and change. Now is the time for radical honesty.

Chapter 2

Fooling Ourselves

We've All Got Skin in the Game

In 2006, I was talking to my husband on my cell phone while pacing around my cul-de-sac. I was trying to convince him that we needed to buy this huge house on a couple of acres up in the mountains that some friends of ours were moving out of. They were in the process of a very messy divorce, and amid everything, they had given up maintaining the house or paying the mortgage. They were headed into bankruptcy. It was a risky investment, buying a 5,000-square-foot home that needed a lot of work, but the market was booming, and we were hoping to fix it up and flip it for double what we paid. We had remodeled several homes by this point, so we were feeling confident.

About a year in, we realized just how bad our decision was. The house was in much worse shape than we anticipated, and because it was so large, it was taking forever to renovate. It was also costing a fortune. When the housing market crashed in 2008, we had the terrible realization that even after we had finished the remodel, we would only be able to sell it for our purchase price. We ended up selling the home seven years later.

During those seven years, we spent every spare moment fixing the house. It robbed us of our rest for so long that we grew to detest the house. By the time we sold it in 2014, the house was gorgeous, but we lost $200,000 in the process. There were a lot of conditions I could blame for this unfortunate life lesson, but the reality is that I made some critical judgment errors in buying the house. My excitement of having a huge house in the mountains clouded my ability to see the situation clearly.

When we find ourselves in a hole, it's instinctive to search for reasons outside of ourselves that explain how we got there. Once I realized we were financially negative on the house, it was easy to blame the market, the mortgage industry for allowing us to extend ourselves so much, my husband for taking too long on the remodel, the previous owners for not disclosing information, and on and on and on.

Conveniently, this type of scapegoating lets me off the hook for my role in the whole mess. If I'm honest with myself, I was the one pushing for the house. I was the one whose ego wanted to have a big, beautiful house to throw parties in. It was I who applied for the mortgage, which was a stretch to afford. I was not a victim. The choices I made were very much the reason we were in over our heads.

When we allow ourselves to blame someone or something else for the lives we have, we lose our ability to determine our future. Scapegoat thinking does not harness the experiential knowledge needed to learn and avoid repeat mistakes.

This chapter is all about uncovering how we have fooled ourselves or have been fooled.

Let me make this disclaimer: taking ownership of our choices is gut-wrenching stuff. Our egos may deflate. We've all got some apologizing to do. We've been part of systems or decisions that have harmed others. We've also been a part of things that have helped others. No one gets out of this one unscathed, so the best we can do is to acknowledge our ignorance and errors and give ourselves a lot of grace to learn and change.

Towering is vital in this process. We have to continually step back and see the big picture. How can we remove the shame, regret, ego, anger, and disappointment to see the part we played without reverting to tunneling either into our old ways or just digging a new one?

The Truth is Technicolored

I used to believe that the truth was absolute. Everything was black and white for me. I even have a tattoo covering my arm that says, "There is no power against the truth." Which I still believe is factual, but I interpret it differently now than when I first sat in the tattoo chair. Now, instead of thinking that there is no power against the truth, I am more inclined to think that there is no power against *your* truth.

Marketers and sales professionals understand that you can't argue with personal experience. This is why they use testimonials to promote things. Like beliefs, we assume someone else's experience will be the same as ours, so we buy the product or idea. But if it doesn't work like we were told, the next time it comes up, we are quick to dismiss it because we have had a personal experience that negates the claims. As Dale Carnegie said, "A man convinced against his will, is of the same opinion still."

When we've learned something through personal experience, it takes a new personal experience to convince us otherwise.

I'm not saying there are no absolute truths; there most certainly are. There are laws of nature, like the way energy is always moving or how we are attracted to things and people like us. There are natural laws of rhythm and for every cause, there is an effect. We cannot deny that these are fundamental and absolute truths to which the whole of humanity is subject.

Here's the caveat, though: we each experience these truths differently because of our limited perspective. I may see some effects of my decisions, but I most certainly won't be able to see all of the impacts. It's like remembering a childhood story with a group of old friends, and although the event was the same, you all had different memories and takeaways.

We are naïve to the experiences and perspectives of others. There's no shame in this. How can we know what we have not known? The cure for ignorance and better decision-making is to include other perspectives with lived experiences.

When I made friends who had political or social views that were different from mine, I realized that they had come to their convictions in the same way I had, through personal experience. My "pull yourself up by the bootstraps" worked well for me and my friends who had boots, but that type of thinking was irrelevant for my friends who didn't have boots.

When I went back to school for my Doctorate in law and policy, I spent the first year beating myself up for my ignorance. It was incredibly hard to be faced with all the assumptions I had made and perspectives I had missed. My peers had such a different take and experience than I did on each of the legal policies we studied.

Their experiences left me in a continual state of contemplation. How they thought was not the way I had been told they thought, and it certainly wasn't the way I had assumed they thought. But there was no way I could have had that experience without being close to them and without respecting their experience and perspective. Proximity to others gives us a new perspective, which adds color to our black and white pallet.

Let the world be more technicolored than black and white. It's prettier that way. But stay away from gray. Gray is for the lazy. It allows us to dull vibrant opinions. Variety is what makes life interesting, so let different colors be different colors. Contrary to our strong desire to have an answer for everything or eliminate any complexity in our lives, it does ourselves and others an injustice when we pigeonhole or categorize everything.

Polarized thinking shrinks the soul. It's okay not to know what you think definitively about issues. Many things can be true at one time, and it's so much better to be able to articulate the different positions and spark thoughtful conversations than to be a self-appointed pundit regurgitating everything you've heard.

A good starting place is to ask yourself:

- Have I sought out all opposing arguments?
- Who believes like I do, and why?
- Who doesn't believe like me, and why?
- Can I intelligently explain why they feel as they do?
- Can I acknowledge that their perspective is as valuable as mine?

Are You Sure?

Confident people are extremely attractive. It's one of the biggest factors in how we choose our leaders. No one wants to follow someone who doesn't come across like they know what they are doing. That said, have you ever met one of those guys who comes across like he's god's greatest gift to mankind, and you scratch your head, wondering, "Where on earth did he get this confidence from?"

For those who are trying to rule the world, bold claims are a powerful tactic. The ability to convince others is a drug for leader types, and I know because I am one. I can't help myself. I'm a walking sales ad about anything I like, always trying to persuade others, even when I don't know I'm doing it. It's a running joke in my family that I can't get a compliment on something I'm wearing without telling the person complimenting me what I paid for it and where they can buy it. I've tried to just say "thank you," but I can't. I want them to know that they can get the same amazing deal I did.

The root of this is my core belief that if someone says they like something, I assume they want to own it. This is a pretty big assumption on my part. It could be that they just want to like it, but I don't even see that as an option most of the time. My extreme confidence levels have convinced me that others think like I do. I like feeling confident, and most of the time, I see it as a huge strength. Unlike knowing where I got an outfit and how much I paid, my confidence in things I don't know for sure can be a very large blind spot. **Everyone wants to feel right, but needing to be right is a trap.**

My husband, Kris, was the first person to really call me on my bullshit. I can honestly say that I didn't even realize how much bullshitting I did until he pointed it out. Like any confident yet inexperienced young person, I had a lot of baseless opinions. When I was trying to convince him of something, I would use absolute language like "always" and "never," or use statistics I couldn't prove. It was much easier before the internet. Now, anyone can fact-check you by searching the web, even thought it is filtered through an algorithm biased toward what they like. Back then, we relied on books and other people's word.

Kris was tired of being bulldozed by my unfounded claims. I would be so surprised when he would ask me things like, "Where is your proof of that?" Proof? I had never been asked for proof. As a natural born leader, I always viewed being confident as more important than being accurate. Plus, I like to get my way, and confidence is a great way to do that. It's the whole "fake it until you make it" phenomenon.

Annie Duke is one of my favorite authors on decision-making. Her book *Thinking In Bets* helped me learn how to think and communicate differently. She likens our communication to playing poker. Our statements of belief are a bet we are making, given the information that we have. We create our beliefs according to what we think has the greatest likelihood of being true; however, it's still a bet. There are still factors we don't know.

Annie Duke helped me see that the reason I was claiming to be 100% right all the time was because I viewed anything less than 100% right as 100% wrong. This is ridiculous, of course, but don't you do this as well? When we recall something that didn't turn out like we wanted, we judge the entire decision as wrong. A more honest assessment is that what happened was a result of many factors and that we made our decisions based on limited understanding.

As a college professor, I dislike true/false and multiple-choice test questions. I find that creating these types of questions forces me to dumb down the information and remove any details so that in every student's mind, there is an obvious right answer. Fundamentally, this is a terrible way to assess a student's understanding of the subject. A superior test of knowledge is a rigorous discussion, essay, or student presentation. It's a better representation of how we come to conclusions. We go back and forth, giving different facts and their own values that add up to one choice or the other being more compelling.

Summarizing our thoughts or defending our opinions is a much better indication of what we are learning because it includes the context for why something may be right or wrong. In reality, we usually don't get a list of options to choose from, with one clearly right answer to the issues we face. Presenting our learning or opinions without all of the caveats we weighed along the way is a terrible way for us to assess and communicate our own beliefs.

We can assess our own beliefs by thinking about how sure we are in a percentage or scale. Stuck in my binary mindset of 100% right or 100% wrong, I didn't give myself the space to evaluate how sure I was about the things I was saying. I needed to feel 100% right all the time because the alternative in my mind was being completely wrong, even if I was only partially wrong or unsure. I didn't understand that we are all making bets on the future.

When I stopped to ask myself how sure I was that my opinion would prove out, my language changed, and it softened my ridged edges. The craziest phenomenon occurred when I changed my speech to better reflect how sure I was instead of convincing myself and others that I was right. I became more confident, not less.

I had a friend come to me once, perplexed about why her husband wasn't interested in having sex. I immediately launched into how if he wasn't interested in sex with her, he must be getting it some other way because what man doesn't have an insatiable sexual appetite? I didn't know this guy very well, so although my own experience led me to this assumption, it was an assumption. I didn't really know.

Instead of getting her all freaked out that he was some philanderer, I should have said, "Wow, that's got to be hard. Have you talked to him about it? That hasn't been my experience or what I've heard from my friends, but there could be reasons; just talk to him about it." If I felt strongly about it, I could have even said something like, "If I was a betting person, I would be 70% confident betting on the idea that something is going on, but that's just me." Instead of, "He's definitely messing around."

It turned out that he had undiagnosed Type 2 Diabetes, and it was killing his sex drive. That's not something that I would have even considered because I hadn't had experience with that. The point is that now I am more aware of just how much I don't have experience with, and I'm a better friend when I factor my ignorance into my advice.

It's a lot of pressure to feel like you have to be right all the time. Assigning a percentage of certainty to the various beliefs and opinions we have relieves some of that pressure and gives us more room to grow and learn. Adam Grant uses an excellent tactic to create space to change our minds in his book *Think Again*. He recommends making a list of conditions that would need to occur for us to change our minds. Making a list of conditions permits us to be flexible in our thinking.

Your Bias is Showing

We are all biased, even though sometimes we don't notice when our bias is showing. We might have an explicit bias that is observable to others, but most of the time, our bias is implicit and subconscious. It's near impossible to get rid of all biases, as there are psychological and scientific reasons we have them, but we must recognize the part they play in our lives.

My own biases about people became more obvious to me when I started looking for a mobile app designer on Upwork. I like to hire experts for my tech work through Upwork or Fiverr because I've had positive experiences finding contractors there, and it also limits my management time.

So, I put the job out there and received nearly a hundred proposals from contractors wanting to do app development. There were a lot of initial proposals to look at, so I started making my first round of eliminations. What I realized about my process had me half-laughing and half-cringing twenty minutes in.

My first filters eliminated anyone who didn't have a perfect 100% score on completed jobs, hadn't made at least $50k doing the work, wasn't rated as being a top contractor on Upwork, and anyone representing a large firm. Here's what this told me about myself: I'm not willing to give someone a chance who is new to the platform, even if they have been rated as a rising talent. I've assumed that if they are decent at their job, they've made enough money at it to survive. I also have an affinity for working with independent business owners instead of large firms.

In my second round of eliminations, I began looking at their profiles and eliminated anyone who didn't take the time to customize their proposal for my job, used a bunch of emojis in their descriptions, or had a cringy profile picture. There were far more men submitting proposals than women, so I gave all the ladies at least double my review time in hopes that I could use them instead of a man. Women supporting women and all.

I purposely hadn't indicated an hourly wage on my job posting, so the proposals were all over the map. I was much less concerned about their hourly wage and more concerned with how many hours they logged on jobs similar to mine. Some people say they want $30 an hour, but it takes them three times longer than someone charging $60 an hour. Where am I going with all of this? If I analyzed my behavior during this process, I'd see a ton of biases.

I'm sure that psychologists have given every type of bias we display an official name. Sometimes, naming or diagnosing a behavior is helpful, and other times, it blurs what is already clear in our hearts and minds. I find that having a name for a behavior assists me in being able to talk about it and relate to others. What once felt like a very individual understanding has now been exposed as a shared human experience.

In my example of considering proposals on Upwork, I can easily identify some of my biases. I could say that I love rooting for the underdog, and that's why I want to give female contractors more consideration, or I could call it gender bias. I could say that I would rather work with a small business owner than a large corporation because I want personalized attention, or I could just acknowledge that I have an affinity bias for small business owners because I am one. I could say that I'm doing my due diligence by comparing the average time it takes a contractor to finish a job, or I could acknowledge that in my professional experience, I've established an anchor bias that I'm comparing to.

An anchoring bias or "anchoring" is when you've had an experience with what something costs or how long it takes to do something, so when you face a similar situation in the future, you compare the cost or time of the new endeavor to what you've known. Anchoring is one of the biases I am most easily fooled by in my own life because it's so prevalent I don't notice it occurring.

For example, last Christmas, I needed to get a new fake Christmas tree. I hadn't started shopping for one, but I happened to see one at Costco when I was doing my weekly grocery run. Now, I'll admit that I have an affinity bias to products that Costco sells because the high quality of the products they sell has been proven to me on many occasions (confirmation bias). So here I am, walking in the door, and there is a Christmas tree for sale for $999! That seemed outrageously expensive to me. I couldn't recall spending anywhere near that before, so I chalked it up as crazy inflation.

I didn't purchase the tree at Costco that day because I didn't want to afford it. It bothered me that I would have to pay a grand for a stupid tree.

Non-coincidentally, I had just finished reading Ariely and Kreisler's behavioral economics book *Dollars and Sense: How We Misthink Money and How to Spend Smarter*, a few days before. The book explained how we anchor when it comes to what we think products should cost, and it's usually based on the first price we see from a reputable seller. Aha, I thought, maybe I'm anchoring because I saw the tree at Costco, and it's been a while since I shopped for a fake Christmas tree. I should double-check if this is the average cost of a new tree instead of assuming that it is. Sure enough, I went to Amazon and put in the specifics of the tree I wanted. Lo and behold, the average price was $400, which was close to what I had remembered paying years ago. Now, I'm sure that the tree at Costco was excellent in some way that I could not have cared less about, but maybe it was just overpriced because there are a ton of people like me who anchor to the pricing of products at Costco or another store we like.

What's my point? We all have biases, and most of them are simply based on what we like or experience and have nothing to do with evil thoughts that want to oppress or harm others through discrimination. We are all just trying not to screw up our lives by using our past hard-won wisdom. In most situations, it is impossible not to be biased, but we do ourselves a disservice when we don't slow down long enough to identify why we are acting in a way that may be more harmful than helpful.

Biases are important to identify in our relationship decisions because they usually come from an intense personal experience. If we've been burned by someone recently, that recency bias can make us project that experience onto others when they don't deserve it. If we've had a positive interaction with someone, we may assume that others with similar qualities will look out for us when we don't have any experience with them that would warrant our trust in them.

How do we navigate this? We can be honest with ourselves about the biases we have and why we have them. We can't allow person-specific biases to become discrimination against an entire group of people. We must afford every person we interact with the opportunity to establish a rapport with us on their own merit, just as we would want them to do with us.

Don't be a Tension Hater

If there's ever been a tension hater, it's me. If I'm given the choice, I will choose confrontation with someone over unspoken tension nearly every time. It's been the struggle of my lifetime to learn the subtle art of keeping my mouth shut and mastering graceful resolve. I would venture to say that most people are the opposite. Confrontation is usually one of those activities people want to avoid like the plague, even if it causes tension in the relationship.

Self-confrontation is a different struggle, but we hate it all the same. It is easier to avoid confronting ourselves because we don't need anyone else to corroborate the lies we tell ourselves. Our brains so badly want to relieve inner tension that we will go to any length to resolve it, even if it means fooling ourselves so that we feel better.

There are three main ways we try to resolve inner tension: we can numb it, fake it, or fix it.

All three of these are a balm for that inner struggle, but only one solves the problem, while the other two just kick the can down the road. When we don't have the internal tools to handle inner tension, we usually resort to numbing it. If things aren't the way we need them to be and we can't see a way to change the situation, a numbing balm is easy to find and quick to bring temporary relief. We might numb with prescriptions or recreational drugs, alcohol, excessive sleep, food, sex, thrill-seeking, or anything else we find that works for us. It's the reason you find yourself ordering chili cheese fries when you are stressed because your credit card is maxed out.

Numbing it. Numbing is useful sometimes, like having a drink to take the edge off when you are at a party with a bunch of people who make you uncomfortable. It's tempting to numb ourselves so that we don't have to confront what's bothering us. But we disable our future selves when we use it as our main tactic for resolving inner tension.

Ignoring your inner tension is like not using your arm because your shoulder is sore. It feels better to stop using it temporarily, and it may even be good to disable it for a short time, but if it's out of use for too long, you end up with an arm that doesn't work right. Physical therapy and doing the hard work of healing would have been a better option. You were built to be able to handle inner tension. Whatever your inner tension is, it's bothering you because something needs to be addressed. Don't disable yourself by not dealing with it.

Faking it. The other way we fool ourselves into resolving inner tension is by faking a resolution. We do this by changing our narrative about the situation to make ourselves feel better. This psychological phenomenon is our effort to eliminate cognitive dissonance. Cognitive dissonance is when we have inconsistent or conflicting thoughts and behaviors, so we alleviate the tension by changing how we feel about one of them.

As a simple example, let's say I want to stop eating sugar, but I love eating candy. These desires conflict, so when I want to eat sugar, I tell myself things like, "It's impossible not to eat sugar, it's in everything!" or "One candy bar won't matter." I know I'm not alone in this.

A more poignant example would be if I like this guy, but he's a huge jerk to me sometimes, so I tell myself that it's because he's tortured or misunderstood. I think I just need to love him better. Turns out I'm just falling for an asshole.

Fixing it. I recognize the self-deception by asking myself, "How would I hear this excuse if someone else were saying it in front of me and it wasn't an issue *I* struggled with?" Nearly 100% of the time I can see my delusion and work to come back toward reality. If it's an excuse, it's an excuse and I'm just trying to make myself feel cozy instead of healthy. I can't imagine a time when our default will be tension-loving, but progress is recognizing the traps of being a tension-hater and working toward true resolve whenever possible.

Quit being your emotion's bitch

Let's come to this one head-on. **You are not your emotions. You are not your feelings. They belong to you. You don't belong to them.** Don't get it twisted.

It is critical that as women, we understand our emotions. For centuries, our emotional intelligence, aka our superpower, has been misunderstood. They used to call being overly emotional or frenzied hysteria. Hysteria was a clinical diagnosis until 1980. The word hysteria was derived from the Greek word for a woman's uterus, or "hystera." Hence, the removal of the uterus is a hysterectomy.

The ancient Greeks and Egyptians believed that a woman's uterus floated around in her belly and created pressure that caused this hysteria. In their very finite wisdom, they deemed one of the solutions for stabilizing the floating uterus to be lots of male semen, preferably within the confines of marriage. You can't make this shit up. If this isn't proof that every system we interact with has been designed or influenced through the filter of the male ego, I don't know what does.

The reality, of course, is much less sensational. Women are emotionally intelligent beings, generally aware of how they feel, and usually more prompt to express it than their male counterparts. We aren't hysterical.

Emotions are simply warning lights. They tell us that we need to take action. If we are feeling anxious, it may mean that something needs closure. If we feel mad, it may mean that we need to confront something. If we feel sad, it may mean we need to grieve or have a conversation. Tunneling is easy when we are highly charged. We want to double down and dig in like a tick, not having further input on why we feel the way we do. Towering is more important than ever when we are feeling emotionally charged because we need to step back, breathe, and take a look at the full landscape.

We women usually have a keen sense when reading the room, seeing behind the smiling facades, and empathizing with others. A man may try to avoid an emotional breakdown by joking about something that happened to them, but a woman is more likely to want to process the grief. The shadow side of our superpower is that sometimes we believe the power *is* us. This means that **sometimes we misinterpret our emotions to be integral to our personality or current situation instead of simply an illuminator for our current situation.** And when we do this, we are at risk of managing our decisions and relationships incorrectly.

When our kids hit their early teens, they confessed to us that they had smoked weed. I completely freaked out. My emotional state went off the rails. Instead of the situation prompting me to see my feelings of anger and betrayal as a warning sign that I was afraid and needed to deal with the news calmly, I became completely irrational. I accused myself of being the worst parent in the world and wanted to have myself committed because I felt suicidal. I thought my kids were drug addicts.

I am so ashamed of how I acted during that time. I became completely ridiculous, given the situation. I tunneled HARD. I overreacted in their punishment and was at serious risk of jeopardizing my long-term relationship with them. My husband was as upset as I was, so he wasn't much help. Luckily, my sons had more sense than I and were able to help me see that although I was trying to make the situation all about me and my parenting, it wasn't. It was about them doing something that (I know now) was fairly common for kids their age, and my overreaction was proving that I wasn't safe for them to confide in.

Am I saying that I shouldn't have punished them? No, I just shouldn't have made it about me. I should have kept it about them, with limited analysis of my parenting, instead of all about how what they did affected *my ego* and how *I* would look to others.

When we let emotions go untethered, we judge incorrectly, leading us to act incorrectly. What I needed to understand at the time was that my anger and betrayal were just fear and lack of control. If I towered and recognized that these things were what was driving my response, I could have addressed things correctly and put in place fitting punishment and controls without escalating the situation to atom-bomb status.

Now would be the perfect time to ask yourself, "What am I angry about? Is it rooted in fear?" Many times, our fear is related to lack of control. Instead of getting angry, say, "This is scary," and see how it changes the dynamic.

Brenee Brown's book, *Atlas of the Heart*, does a beautiful job of discussing the roots of emotions. In it, she explains why we get upset when someone is lying on the couch while we are feverishly picking up before a guest comes over. It is because we are envious that they feel comfortable NOT picking up. We want others to view things with the same importance we do, and when they don't, we experience envy, which makes us mad because we have placed a sense of duty on ourselves, and they have not. There's also the huge issue of us not ever wanting to look bad.

When I was reading *Atlas of the Heart*, I had an "aha" moment. When I was a younger mom, I became very judgmental and upset at a friend of mine who, also being a mother, did not change her youthful, pre-mom activities. She was still going out often and hanging out with her friends. I judged her behavior so harshly. Only twenty-five years later did I realize that the reason her actions upset me so much was because she had not given up her independence and freedom like I had, and I was jealous.

I wasn't jealous of the going out; I was jealous that she had kept that part of herself alive, and I had given up more of myself than I wanted to admit. I was only able to come to this revelation because one of the questions in Brenee's book was to ask yourself who you resent. I couldn't think of anyone off the top of my head, so I asked myself, "Who have you ever resented?" This took me back to all the years I had resented this person.

I began to wonder why I used to resent them but didn't anymore. I realized that I didn't resent them anymore because I felt free to live the life I want to live, and back then, I did not. I don't resent her anymore because I am doing what I want to do, but for all those years, I was jealous of her sense of freedom. I was mad she hadn't taken the martyr role like I had. What I had thought was justified judgment was mostly just jealousy. I completely misunderstood why I was feeling the way I was.

Remember, forgiveness is always for your freedom. It's not for the person you forgive. It's for you. Harboring resentment and bitterness only robs you of your freedom.

Now is the time to ask yourself, "Who do I resent or have ever resented?" Find your inner four-year-old and keep asking why, why, why until you get to the root of your resentment. Make peace with why you felt the way you felt, identify it, and root it out more quickly going forward. If you acted on that resentment by treating someone badly, it is time to make amends for your freedom's sake.

Don't Lie to Yourself about What You Want

In 2018, I came to an alarming realization about myself. I didn't want to be who I was supposed to be. Let me explain. One day, I read something that resonated so deeply and explained my life in such a way that there was no going back for me. Oddly enough, it came from the German philosopher Friedrich Nitzsche, famous for his criticism of Christianity. I was a Christian pastor at the time, so I'm not sure if I was reading it to be able to discount it or if I just happened to stumble upon it in my schoolwork. Either way, it hit me like a ton of bricks, and I could not shake my newfound clarity.

Now, I'm not a Nietzsche expert, and I certainly can't promote everything he wrote or represented during his time on Earth, but some key takeaways may be relevant to you. Nietzsche, like me, was raised as a pastor's kid. He grew up highly critical of systems he felt were hypocritical. He had a whole lot to say about the Christian ideals of asceticism, which is the denial of worldly pleasures and desires. Nietzsche taught that the denial of our passion and desires can be destructive if we allow it to excuse us from the life we were meant to live.

In his book, *On the Genealogy of Morality*, he describes how downtrodden people groups develop a type of morality that helps explain away the oppression. This re-wording of their plight gives them the mental upper hand so that they can cope and not feel mad at the world all the time. For example:

- An oppressed person may decide that their submission is noble for the greater good.
- A poor person may decide that having money must be the byproduct of evil deeds and greed because they are a good person, but don't have any.
- A person who feels like they can't change their life may decide that meekness is more honorable than power.
- A sick person might claim that they are well because that's what it takes to have faith.
- A lazy person might say that they are waiting for guidance.
- A person who has a hard time asserting themselves may decide that humility at all times is the better way.

Nietzsche contends that these are all ways we fool ourselves into believing that we are doing something righteous, but what we are doing is denying our true desires. For what other reason would we need to identify our complacency as a virtue?

I remember being stunned. It felt like someone had been reading my mail. I was part of an oppressive church governance structure that only allowed me to be a supporter of the men in leadership. Still, I kept telling myself it was acceptable because it's how those in authority interpreted the Bible. I was happily married to a man who respected me, but we were still playing by the rules that, somehow, he had the authority over our household.

I am an entrepreneur and good at making money, but I didn't feel I could pursue that in the way I wanted because it would cross over into greed or some other ugly trait. Although I'm a natural leader, I often felt I had to follow someone less qualified than me because that was my role as a woman. If I was doing well or feeling happy, that needed to be subdued because some people around me weren't doing well, and my job was to make sure they got better before I could enjoy my life. Martyrdom was venerated in my world.

It wasn't just me, though. As I sat there contemplating the ways I had fooled myself with these oppressions I had re-titled to be virtues, I realized that many of the people closest to me had fallen into the same trap, ruining their lives. They were stuck in unhappy and oppressive marriages and tried to make themselves feel better by holding on to the nobility of their submission. They were financially broke and weren't even trying to dig themselves out because it was easier to say they trusted God with their finances. It goes on and on. We fool ourselves by not being honest about what it takes to get what we want or be who we want to be. I'm not advocating for selfishness, but I am opposed to oppression. It is possible to follow your dreams without harming those you love.

The Future You Will Thank You

Like I said at the beginning of this chapter, we've all got some owning up to do. Truth brings growth, and growth is good. Visualize your future self who isn't so easily fooled by her voice. Act where there needs to be action. Remember that there is no such thing as standing still in life. Not working toward what you want and who you want to be is a decision to let life pass you by. You don't have to untangle yourself overnight. Small steps in the direction you want to go brings big results. Be a person of integrity. Ask yourself if your actions will produce the person you want to be. If you see inconsistencies in your life, do the hard work of dealing with them and move toward the vision of the life you want. You've got this!

Building Blocks

- When we allow ourselves to blame someone or something else for the lives we have, we lose our ability to determine our future. Scapegoat thinking does not harness the experiential knowledge needed to learn and avoid repeat mistakes.

- When we've learned something through personal experience, it takes a new personal experience to convince us otherwise.

- Proximity to others gives us a new perspective, which adds color to our black and white thinking.

- Everyone wants to feel right, but needing to be right all the time is a trap.

- It's a trap to express your opinion as being 100% right because it automatically means you were 100% wrong when you need to correct a mistake. Allow yourself to express your confidence on a scale.

- It is impossible not to be biased, but we do ourselves a disservice when we don't slow down long enough to identify why we are acting in a way that may be more harmful than helpful.

- There are three main ways we try to resolve inner tension: we can numb it, fake it, or fix it.

- You are not your emotions. You are not your feelings. They belong to you. You don't belong to them.

- Sometimes, we misinterpret our emotions to be integral to our personality or current situation instead of simply being an illuminator for our current situation.

- Resentment reveals what and who we envy.

- Forgiveness is for your freedom, not theirs.
- The denial of our passion and desires can be destructive if we allow it to excuse us from the life we were meant to live.

Toolkit

Chapter 2: Fooling Ourselves

Q1. We are good at fooling ourselves. Think of a time when you were fooled. In what ways can you take ownership of that?

_____
_____
_____
_____

Q2. Being around people with a different perspective or lived experience helps us see the world differently. Think of a situation or two where you changed your opinion because someone you were close to had a different experience than you.

_____
_____
_____
_____

Q3. It's a lot of pressure to feel like you have to be right all the time. Assigning a percentage of certainty to the various beliefs and opinions we have relieves some of that pressure and gives us more room to grow and learn. Think of a couple of strong opinions you have. Assign a percentage of confidence to those opinions. How does this confidence percentage change the way you will communicate this opinion?

_____
_____
_____
_____

Q4. We all have biases. Most of our biases are simply based on what we like or experience and have nothing to do with evil thoughts that want to oppress or harm others through discrimination. We are all just trying not to screw up our lives by using our past hard-won wisdom. In most situations, it is impossible not to be biased, but we do ourselves a disservice when we don't slow down long enough to identify why we are acting in a way that may be more harmful than helpful. Think of an area in your life or relationship that you would like to improve. What biases are at play there? How are they affecting your decision-making?

_____
_____
_____
_____

Q5. There are three main ways we try to resolve inner tension: we can numb it, fake it, or fix it. In what ways have you numbed your inner tension by ignoring it or using a substance to avoid it?

_____
_____
_____
_____

Q6. Cognitive dissonance is when we have inconsistent or conflicting thoughts and behaviors, so we alleviate the tension by changing how we feel about one of them. How have you tried to resolve inner tension by faking a resolution this way?

_____
_____
_____
_____

Q7. Emotions are simply warning lights. They tell us that we need to take action. If we are feeling anxious, it may mean that something needs closure. If we feel mad, it may mean that we need to confront something. If we feel sad, it may mean we need to grieve or have a conversation. Sometimes we misinterpret our emotions as integral to our personality or current situation instead of simply an illuminator for our current situation. In what ways have you allowed yourself to be bossed around by your emotions?

_____
_____
_____
_____

Q8. Many times, our fear is related to not having control. What are you angry about that is rooted in fear? How does reframing your anger as a fear response change its power over you?

_____
_____
_____
_____

Q9. Who do you resent? Why do you resent them? Can you identify elements of envy in your resentment?

_____
_____
_____
_____

Q10. Nietzsche's philosophy is that these are all ways we fool ourselves into believing that we are doing something righteous, but what we do is deny our true desires. In what ways have you lied to yourself about your desires under the cloak of virtue?

_____
_____
_____
_____

The Truth is Technicolored Exercise

Variety is what makes life interesting. Contrary to our strong desire to have an answer for everything or eliminate any complexity in our lives, it does ourselves and others an injustice when we need to pigeonhole or categorize everything. It's ok not to know what you think definitively about an issue. It's so much better to be able to articulate the different positions and spark thoughtful conversations than regurgitate what you've always thought.

Think of a topic you have a strong opinion about. Now ask yourself these questions:

Have I sought out all opposing arguments?

_____
_____

Who believes like I do, and why?

_____
_____

Who doesn't believe like me, and why?
_____
_____

Can I explain intelligently why they feel as they do?
_____
_____

Can I acknowledge that their perspective is as valuable as mine?
_____
_____

Chapter 3

You Can Only Own What's Yours

Most women I know have a control freak side. Some of us are a little freaky on all of our sides. It just presents differently. We pick and choose what we want to take control of. These choices have everything to do with what we believe to be ours. Because control has been such a pinnacle desire in my life, I often get existential about it, attempting to analyze when and why I want control over areas in my life. The answer is that we erect our center of control where we believe it will be most effective, our territory.

Your Territory

You are born with a sense of self. You discover within the first few months of life that your hands and feet belong to you and can be controlled by you. When you start to talk, you learn the word "mine" very quickly. We are territorial creatures by nature. We want to know that we have agency over our own lives. This ability to have a say, our agency, is one of the primary drives as humans.

We hate being told what to do so much that there's a theory for our hatred of it: reactance theory. When we feel pressured by someone, even if it's something we may be interested in, the external pressure will make us want to do the opposite just to prove that we have our own will. That is reactance theory.

Our desire for control runs so deep that we will even self-sabotage or harm ourselves because we feel these actions are at least in our control. It's the reason we see kids who were raised in extremely strict environments rebel. It's why partners who feel trapped look for secret ways of escaping the relationship through affairs. It's why those who feel powerless in real-life revel in the comfort of speaking out anonymously online. We hate feeling powerless, and we will find a way to have some semblance of territorial control.

Understanding Control

Let's look at the lives of two different women, Claire and Darlene.

Claire was raised by two parents and had many siblings. Her parents worked hard, but they lived paycheck to paycheck. She shared a room and clothes with her sisters. Hardly anything in her life was just hers. Claire experienced all of the normal stages of growing up. She went to her first dance, had her first kiss, and played sports. When she was fifteen, her hockey coach sexually assaulted her when taking her home from practice one day. He often took her home because both of her parents worked a lot, and she couldn't drive yet. Although she was able to get out of the car, the incident left Claire feeling scared and confused. Her coach was an old high school friend of her dad's, whom she had known most of her life. She didn't think her parents would believe her if she said anything, and sometimes, she even felt like she must have imagined it or done something to give him the wrong idea.

For a couple of weeks after the assault, she feigned illness to get out of school and practice, but she knew she couldn't do that forever. She tried talking to her mom about wanting to drop out of hockey, but her mom dismissed her and reminded her that she was the best one on the team and had a real chance at getting a full-ride scholarship to college. Claire knew her parents couldn't afford to pay for college, and she really wanted to go, so she figured out a way to live in the tension. She found other rides home and made sure she was never alone with her coach, but she could feel herself withdrawing. Claire became even more disciplined than she was before. She started weightlifting more, eating less, and spending her free time doing schoolwork. Her parents noticed that she was getting skinnier and more sullen, but chalked it up to teenage insecurity. After all, she was doing better in school and hockey than ever.

Internally, Claire was spiraling. She felt alone and vulnerable. It felt like she couldn't control the course of her life. She was adjusting her life to avoid her coach, working out like crazy so that she would feel strong if something happened again, and for a reason she couldn't understand, she started to vomit her food after she ate because it made her feel better. If you were to ask Claire how she felt during those high school years, she would have told you that she felt voiceless and scared.

Claire did get the scholarship. She went to college, got married, and had a couple of kids. She became what some would call a helicopter mom. She coddled and hovered. There was no way in hell she was going to allow what happened to her to happen to them. When her kids got their first phones in junior high, she tracked their locations and copied herself on every text. Her husband and kids often complained about her controlling nature, but she always fired back that she was just lovingly protecting them.

Claire grew up feeling ownership over a very small territory, and the only areas she felt control over were her actions, her body, and her bunk bed. As she got older and had a family of her own, her territory grew to include them, and her expression of love presented itself as protective control. Claire's self-harm growing up and overwhelming worry as a parent were the byproducts of feeling powerless in other areas.

Just like Claire, **we tend to develop control tactics in the areas we feel we own. The smaller that area is, the more concentrated the control**. We also develop strong boundary lines around our territory because we've learned over time that there are people who are going to try to take what is ours.

Now, let's look at the life of Darlene.

Darlene played hockey with Claire in high school. Her parents divorced when she was little, and she was raised by her dad. Darlene always had her own room as a kid and was allowed to decorate it however she wanted. She felt like she had free reign of the entire house, inviting her friends over every weekend. Darlene's dad was the school district superintendent, and she often saw him at school when he was making his rounds. His status in their small town gave her a sense of belonging, as if she owned a little part of it. Darlene and her dad had a loving relationship, and although he was busy, she knew she could talk to him if she needed to. Darlene had ok grades and wasn't worried about how well she did in hockey. It was just a hobby for her. Darlene had her share of love interests growing up, but none of them were that serious. She was much more interested in just having fun.

Darlene decided to join the Peace Corps right after college and started working as an Executive Director of a non-profit in a large city. She usually saved up her money to spend on big travel excursions with her friends. Darlene was fine with the fact that she would probably never be able to retire and figured the future would take care of itself. She had several long-term relationships, but never really felt the need to tie the knot or have kids. Although sometimes she felt like she was missing out, she was content taking things as they came.

Unlike Claire, Darlene grew up feeling ownership over a large territory. She felt she had free reign in her home, school, and community. From her perspective, the world was her oyster. She didn't feel the need to master any individual area of her life because she felt some control over all of it. Although she knew she was passing up some life experiences, like settling down or having a baby, she didn't know if they were worth the sacrifice of giving up her freedom. Without those constraints, she was able to explore as she wanted. She even chose a profession in non-profit work because it gave her the sense that she could change the world.

Darlene's friends loved her free spirit when they were all younger, but now it was frustrating. She didn't understand that they couldn't abandon everything to on vacation, or go out late when she called at 10 p.m. Darlene started to notice that her friends weren't inviting her over much anymore. She experienced some loneliness, which was expected. When the entire world is your home, it's easy to get lost not knowing your place. It's also easy to enter into someone else's territory without realizing you've crossed a boundary.

We vary in our reactions to what life throws at us. Not everyone who is harmed will react by being overly protective. Some people are harmed so frequently and extremely that it breaks their spirit, and they give up even trying to protect themselves. Not everyone who has a lot of liberty wants it. Some people enjoy structure and seek it out for happiness. No matter how we come to what we establish as our territory, the truth remains that we all have one. Our place. Our people. Our center of control.

Identifying Your Territory

It's helpful to identify what you view as your territory. If Claire had seen that the abuse she suffered effectively shrunk what she felt she could control, she could have recognized her self-harm as a control tactic. Then, she could have found empowerment in different ways. In the same vein, if Darlene had seen that she lacked boundaries, maybe she wouldn't have ruined friendships bulldozing over their boundaries.

So, what is your territory? It is what and who you are ultimately responsible for. If something happened in that place or to those people, the judge would point you as the responsible party.

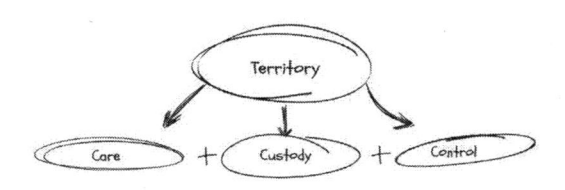

Territory → Care + Custody + Control

I define territory as having the care, custody, and control of an area of your or someone else's life. In the insurance world, it's how we determine responsibility.

Care means that it's your responsibility at that time to care for the property.

Custody means that you are responsible for protecting it.

Control means that you have the power to make decisions about it.

I find this language useful when I'm trying to evaluate what people and possessions are in my territory. When my children were minors and lived in my home, I had care, custody, and control of them. I was legally, financially, physically, and emotionally responsible for them. When they became adults, I no longer had custody or control. They were responsible for their own lives and the decisions they made about them. I didn't give up care because, as a parent, I would still do anything they needed without question, but I was no longer in control because they were healthy and capable adults. I had to let go and let them have their own territory.

If your partner is a healthy adult, they are not personally in your territory. You shouldn't have control over them. However, there are probably areas in your relationship that are part of your territory, depending on the agreements you've made. If you share finances or a house, then you've agreed that your money and home are joint territory. If you have agreed to be monogamous, then your sexual activities are part of that joint territory.

Territory can only be shared by two people when it is owned by two people.

When we don't understand where our territory lies, we are susceptible to making some big mistakes. We make these mistakes when we:

1. Waste time, money, energy, and emotion building on land that isn't ours.
2. Don't tend to our business because we are busy dabbling in someone else's.
3. Trespass into other people's territory.

Trying to fix other people is a fool's errand. We can't Botox someone else's forehead because we're tired of seeing them scowl. We become dumbasses when we spend our hard-earned money renovating a house we rent. We're idiots when we do for others what they refuse to do for themselves. We each get our lot in life. As adults, we get to do what we want with it, which expresses what we value.

Our problem is that in our arrogance, we think that people don't want the life they've made because it's not the life we want for ourselves. Newsflash, we all find a way to get what we want. We may not know why we do the things we do, but deep down, we do them because we believe they will make us happy.

When I was raising teenagers and my kids were becoming young adults, it was really hard to watch them make mistakes because the stakes were higher than when they were young. It was tempting to try to rescue them from the consequences of their mistakes, because who wants to see their child struggle? When they had a mean boss, I wanted to go in and wreak some havoc. When they got a speeding ticket and their insurance rates went up, I wanted to help pay for it because they didn't make much money. My instinct as a mom was to want to rescue them, but when it came to life lessons they needed to learn, rescuing was the worst thing I could do for them.

The universe is always trying to give us what we need for what's next. If we need compassion, the universe will give us a big dose of relatable experience. If we need courage, we will find ourselves in situations where it is required so that we can build it. The universe is so benevolent that if we don't learn the lesson, we will keep getting opportunities to get it right.

When we intervene in someone else's opportunity to learn, we have just made their lives harder. We haven't rescued them. We've delayed their learning and growth. Now they have to go through another hardship because they didn't get what they needed from the experience. It's probably no surprise that being raised as a pastor's kid and being a pastor, I had a severe savior complex. It's still a blind spot for me at times. I never saw it as a problem until I understood my role in complicating the lives of my family through my "saving."

Life's circumstances are not happening to you, they are happening for you. The only reason we even have the power to intervene is because somewhere along the line, we had to learn that lesson. If it's in our territory, it is our lesson to be learned. These lessons are a gift.

Trespassing

Interfering in other people's lives is such a temptation for me that I've had to develop a safe word for myself. I say it to myself every time I want to send a text or make a call that is attempting to intervene where I shouldn't. That word is trespassing. Just the other day, I stopped myself from sending a job opportunity to my daughter because even though I want her to switch jobs, she must not want it because she isn't looking for other jobs. I typed out the text and deleted it as soon as I reminded myself that, in this situation, I was trespassing.

Trespassing means to enter into someone else's territory uninvited. My daughter hadn't asked me to help her look for new jobs, so this was not joint territory. I'm not saying that we shouldn't try to help other people, but help is only helpful when it is wanted. There is a difference between helping and trespassing. We trespass when we give unwelcome advice or leap to defend someone who isn't asking us to. We trespass when we get involved in our friends' fights. We trespass when we speak for someone else who is capable of speaking for themselves. Our intentions aren't malicious. We are just trying to help, but we don't recognize when we've crossed the line. We don't appreciate it when someone else trespasses. Why do we assume they will appreciate our trespassing, no matter how good our intentions are?

There are many ways I struggle with trespassing. My kids sometimes have to correct me when I share news that isn't mine to share on social media. My "proud mom" intentions are good, but if they wanted that out there on social media, they would have posted it themselves. I now ask permission first, which takes it out of the trespassing category. I also trespass when I plead with my girlfriend to leave her emotionally abusive husband. When she complains to me about him and the horrible things he does, I misunderstand her need to vent to a friend as my invitation to offer advice when she hasn't asked for it. I trespass in this situation by trying to solve a problem I haven't been asked to solve. My good intention backfires when I do this because my unwanted advice puts her on the defensive, and she doesn't feel safe talking to me about it anymore. This puts her in an even more vulnerable situation, exactly the opposite of what I wanted to do.

We can become such regular trespassers in certain areas of other people's lives that we are more like squatters than trespassers. This could be not staying in our lane at work by continually trying to do someone else's job. It could also be taking on a protective or maternal role that we weren't asked to play. I've cared for many children over the years as a foster parent. I've learned from those experiences that a child has to want you as a mother figure to be a mother figure. Most of the youth we took care of were older teens, and I was a young woman. It didn't work for me to assert myself as a mothering figure if they just needed me to be a temporary guardian. Finding that balance is a struggle for many foster or step-parents.

Squatters

I've had the very unfortunate experience of learning all about squatter's rights. We own a couple of rental properties, and squatters have become a major issue for landlords across the country. Trespassing is when someone enters your property temporarily. **Squatting** is when they decide to stay and set up the house. This can happen in a couple of different ways. A squatter can enter a vacant house and set up without anyone noticing for a while, or they can transform from being a tenant who was paying their rent to someone who stops paying but refuses to move out. In both situations, they have some legal rights. As if they were lawful tenants, the landlord has to give them legal notice and a timeline to evacuate the premises. If they don't leave, the landlord has to go through a legal eviction process, even though it's the squatters who have broken the law or contract to be there in the first place.

Squatter's rights are part of what's called adverse possession in the real estate world. It's when you take over control of a property that isn't yours. Adverse possession laws will even allow people to eventually take ownership of someone's property if they can prove that they've been there long enough and lived in it as if it were their own. Squatters can live rent-free for as long as it takes to go through the eviction process, which in many cases, takes months.

Why am I talking about squatter's rights? Sometimes, we fool ourselves into thinking that when we've camped out at a territory for a long time, it belongs to us. The classic example of this would be an affair with someone else's partner. If we are the ones having an affair with a married or committed person, they may have invited us into their lives, but their partner probably hasn't, which means we are trespassing. **The trespassing turns into squatting when we view the other party as ours, even when they aren't because they've already**

committed to someone else. If you find yourself squatting, check in on your boundaries. Where is your territory, and where are you trespassing? If you want to develop land, go right ahead, but it's not yours until you own it. Don't foolishly build on someone else's land.

Protecting your territory

There are seasons when we are responsible for the care, custody, and control of kids, clients, sick family members, or elderly parents. In these times, it is our responsibility to protect those that live within our territory. Children under eighteen need a legal guardian because they don't yet have what they need to take care of themselves. Caregiving is a hard and thankless job. There isn't a parent or caregiver out there who hasn't wanted to throw in the towel and say, "Do whatever you want," but prematurely releasing your responsibility is a mistake. Keep showing up. Keep trying. You were given this territory because the universe knew it was meant to belong to you. You have everything you need to handle it. Do what you need to do to guard it.

When you identify your territory, it permits you to set boundaries, to set up flags if you will. For those of us who tend to get our boundaries trampled, it's good practice to name and voice the boundaries you have for yourself and those who you are responsible for. It helps us and those around us know what behavior is acceptable. Without proper or known boundaries, we unintentionally welcome encroachers into our territory.

Encroachment

Encroachment is another real estate concept where a neighbor of yours starts to take over your land by building over the property line. It usually happens unintentionally, but it is encroachment, nonetheless. **Encroachers** are those closest to us that don't realize they've stepped into our territory.

Kris and I did this the other day to our daughter. Her car was totaled after a wreck, so she needed to buy a new one. She doesn't know a lot about cars, but Kris usually helps with that sort of thing. We weren't in the same state, so we started shopping in her price range where we were. We just told her we were doing it without asking her if she wanted us to. It completely stressed her out because she wanted to shop for herself on her timeline. She was able to push back lovingly, but until she did, I hadn't even considered that we were encroaching.

What would have been normal mothering when she was younger, wasn't appropriate given her current stage of life. I hadn't made the mental leap in that area yet. She didn't come right out and tell us we were encroaching, but her reaction to our shopping revealed what we were doing.

It's easy to encroach as women because we have an internal drive to want to know details. Men don't seem to be as interested in the vast amount of information we want about other people. This is evident whenever my husband gets off the phone with a friend who has news, only for him to be grilled about the conversation by me. He knows I will do this and now preemptively warns me that what he is telling me is all he knows so I don't waste time asking him for more details.

Unfortunately for us, sometimes what we want to know isn't really what we need to know. We can encroach by asking for more information than we should. With our kids, it's tempting to want all the nitty-gritty about their lives because we are interested in their well-being and are convinced that our involvement will benefit them. Our involvement isn't always needed or wanted, so stay sensitive to the cues they are giving and let them open up in their own time or keep things private if they wish.

When we are the offending party and we don't realize it, figure it out by watching other people's behaviors instead of waiting for them to say something. Assertive personalities may lash out, but those who are more passive may try to distance themselves from us by telling us less about the areas where we tend to take over. You know your people. Listen to their words and actions and move back to your territory when you are encroaching.

Building Blocks

- We are territorial creatures by nature. We want to know that we have agency over our own lives.
- Your territory is what or who you have care, custody, or control of.
- Territory can only be shared by two people when it is owned by two people.
- We develop control tactics in the areas we feel we own. The smaller that area is, the more concentrated the control.
- By intervening in other people's lives when we shouldn't, we sabotage their learning from the situation and subject them to further pain because they have to go through another situation to learn what they need to learn.
- Trespassing means to enter into someone else's territory uninvited.
- We trespass when we give unwelcome advice.

- We trespass when we leap to defend someone who isn't asking us to.
- We trespass when we get involved in our friends' fights.
- We trespass when we speak for someone else who is capable of speaking for themselves.
- Knowing your territory helps you establish boundaries.
- Squatters are trespassers who have taken up residency.
- We squat when we try to build on someone else's foundation.
- We squat when we take on a role we weren't invited to play in someone's life.
- It's easy to encroach on territory close to us, so we must be conscientious of our neighbors/friends/family's actions and attitudes to help us know when we are offending in this area.

Toolkit

Chapter 3: You Can Only Own What's Yours

Q1. We develop control tactics in the areas we feel we own. The smaller that area is, the more concentrated the control. In what areas are you most controlling?

_____
_____
_____
_____

Territory Exercise

Your territory is what and who you are ultimately responsible for. It's what and who you have care, custody, and control over. Remember that territory can only be shared by more than one person when it is owned by those same people.

- Care means that it's your responsibility at that time to care for the person or property.
- Custody means that you are responsible for the protection of them or it.
- Control means that you have the power to make decisions about them or them.

Who do you have care, custody, and control over and why?

_____
_____

Who have you been claiming that isn't yours? Why?

_____
_____

What do you have care, custody, and control over, and why?

_____
_____

What have you been claiming as yours that isn't? Why?

_____
_____

In what ways have you wasted time, money, energy, and emotion building on land that isn't yours?

_____
_____

In what ways have you neglected your territory because you are busy dabbling in someone else's?

_____
_____

Trespassing means to enter into someone else's territory uninvited. In what ways have you or are you trespassing?

_____
_____

Squatting is when you've been trespassing so long, you think the space belongs to you. In what ways have you or are you squatting in someone else's territory?

_____
_____

In what ways have you failed to protect your territory? How will you protect it going forward?

_____
_____

Encroachers are those closest to us that don't realize they've stepped into our territory. Are there any encroachers in your territory? What boundaries will you put in place to stop this?

_____
_____

Has someone been trying to tell you through their words or actions that you are encroaching on their territory? How will you remind yourself not to do this in the future?

_____
_____

Chapter 4

Martyrdom

Martyrs are made through suffering and giving up their lives for their beliefs. I would consider most of the women I know to dabble in martyrdom at some point. Out of duty and love, we sacrifice the lives we want so that others can live better. It's a noble idea and something we venerate as women. There are times during our lives when it is necessary to sacrifice until it hurts. When raising kids, caring for a sick relative, or assisting aging parents, we step up to the plate knowing it won't be reciprocated anytime soon, but we are happy to do it.

Women are good at giving. Sometimes, it feels so good that we don't know when to stop. It's like we get so comfortable in a sacrificial role that we don't know how to shut it off. We think that the more of ourselves we give, the better a person we are. **News flash–sometimes giving up your life doesn't accomplish the greater good. It just means you have less life.** At the end of the day, no one benefits from your suffering and giving up your life to the point of being a shell of a person.

We women tend to take on a caregiving role. As a gender, we are often the primary caregivers at home, work, and with friends. I don't know about you, but I've never seen my husband arrange a meal train for his buddy who is sick. In fact, 57-81% of caregivers for older people are women across multiple countries (Sharma, Chakrabarti and Grover). There's a debate about the reasons for this. Is it cultural or innate? The answer is both.

Who a woman feels responsible for and for how long is a primarily cultural construct. In 2010, I co-founded and ran a transitional living facility for women and their children. During that time, we had a mother living there from a very different culture than my own. She had some teenage sons she did not feel obligated to control. It was a continual frustration for our team, until we better understood her and her culture. She had been married off by her tribe as a pre-teen and had survived many years of civil war in her country. Her life experience and culture led her to treat her teenage sons as adults even though they weren't considered adults in American culture. Understanding her history and culture helped us manage expectations.

Caretaking is also innate for most women. The nurturing instinct feels natural, but I know that not all women feel that way, nor should they have to. We may assume a caregiving role in some relationships or situations, but not feel that same compulsion in others. For instance, I baby my granddaughter when she's sick, but my husband usually gets a big "suck it up" from me. This instinct to care for everyone around us is one of our superpowers, but it can also be our kryptonite if we aren't careful. This chapter is about avoiding codependency traps and doing what you must do to care for yourself.

There are some common role traps I've noticed in my own life that I've given names to. It's an easy way to remind myself when falling into a trap.

The sheepdog

Do you know how sheep dogs are bred to corral? They ensure everyone around them is ok and migrating forward before they keep going. I've acted like a sheepdog for way too long. It's the trap of waiting for the weakest link before you do what is in your heart to do. I see this in us a lot, like when we are afraid of taking a job that makes more than our partner, not pursuing a credential or degree because it's not valued in our family or community, or not letting ourselves relax until everyone else in the room has everything they could need. It gets so bad that sometimes we can't even let ourselves have a good time because someone close to us is depressed or suffering. I see it when we don't allow ourselves to feel good about where we are at in life because one of our kids is struggling, or when we don't celebrate how good we feel about our bodies because a friend with us is feeling insecure. We do it in so many ways, and it's a trap.

I used to formally counsel and mentor people, so I ended up hearing a lot of other people's problems. If you are a borderline empath like me, that role isn't a great way to keep your spirits up. I would get so bogged down with other people's junk that it affected my ability to be happy. I was serving families struggling with poverty and addiction at work and then counseling youth at different times of the week. It never turned off.

My brother called out my dysfunctional thinking when he pointed out that I was gauging my happiness on how well those around me were doing. He said my outlook on life was dependent on the outlook of others, which is a straight line to depression when you are working with people who are struggling all the time. It took me a long time to process his indictment because I didn't want to admit I was unhealthy. It took even longer for me to understand that I needed to stop waiting for other people to catch up, and move forward.

If there's something positive you need to do for you, do it. You know what it is and why you need to do it. Don't wait for anyone to permit you or champion your idea. At the end of the day, we all get to choose the life we want. You are responsible for yourself, and everyone else is going to do what they want to do. You won't change or stop them, so do it your way and eliminate the excuse of needing to make sure everyone else is pacing with you along the journey.

The proxy

A proxy is someone who represents someone else in a decision or vote. In our efforts to help those we love, we often fall into the proxy trap. It's when we do for others what they will not do for themselves.

Were you ever the girl who helped your friend break up with a guy in middle school because she was afraid to confront him? I was. Have you ever done most of your kid's school projects because you didn't want to say they couldn't go to the birthday party instead of studying? I have. Have you ever looked for jobs for someone who keeps complaining about theirs? Yep, me too. Even if you don't act on their behalf, you may ruminate about their problem more than they do. I can't even count all the sleepless nights I've had over a family member's choices that don't seem to bother them much.

I don't know about you, but I've had the sneaking hunch before that some people in my life haven't learned to do certain things they don't like because they know it will bother me, and I'll do it for them. I'm trying hard to get better at not being a proxy, barring someone's inability to act on their own behalf, because it's not doing them any favors. The truth is, the reason they don't do it themselves is because it isn't important to them. Let that sink in. They don't do it themselves because it is not what they want. If they wanted to do it, they would.

When we act on someone else's behalf, we take away their agency to control their own lives, and that's trespassing. Our actions aren't helpful but harmful.

The cleaner-upper

Everything has a consequence, whether good or bad. Consequences of all types are wonderful. I say bring them on. They are the natural byproduct of our actions and the way we learn. If our goal is to learn and grow from our accomplishments and missteps, we need to appreciate the necessary and helpful role of consequences in our lives. We also need to recognize the essential and useful role they play in the lives of others.

Not long ago, I was talking to a mom who was dealing with the unintended consequences of financially bailing out her adult daughter. Her daughter was used to spending irresponsibly because she knew her mom would pay off her debt if she got in a pickle. The mom wasn't rich, and bailing out her daughter was putting her financial security at risk, but she hated to deny her and the grandkids.

The mom started to notice that the requests for financial help didn't decline. They ramped up. Her daughter just kept spending because now they had developed a pattern. The daughter felt some shame in asking for money repeatedly, but it didn't stop her. The shame drove a wedge in their relationship. The daughter didn't mean to resent the need for her mom's money, but she did and began to distance herself emotionally. The mom didn't mean to resent her daughter asking her for money, but it stung every time her daughter took a trip or bought something unnecessary. What was meant to bring them closer together was backfiring.

Owing someone something changes the nature of a relationship. It moves from a social relationship to a business relationship, even if it's a close family or friend. The lines get blurred, and people begin to act differently toward each other. When someone feels like they are continually the taker or the giver, roles get skewed, and resentment kicks in. Keep this in mind in your zeal to help.

Cleaning up someone else's mess because they don't want to do it limits their learning and growth. Don't do it. In the same way, you wouldn't take credit for the things they got right, don't take responsibility for what they got wrong. Remember, the universe is continually working to teach us what we need for what's next. Don't be the reason they have to go around that mountain again before climbing to the top.

Building Blocks

- Sometimes, giving up your life doesn't accomplish the greater good. It just means you have less life.

- If there's something positive you need to do for you, do it. Don't wait for anyone to permit you or champion your idea. You know what you need to do, and you know why you need to do it.

- We act like sheepdogs while waiting for the weakest link to move forward on our journey.

- We act like a proxy when we do for others what they will not do for themselves.

- Barring someone's inability to act on their own behalf, they don't do it themselves because it isn't essential to them. If they wanted to do it, they would.

- Cleaning up someone else's mess because they don't want to do it limits their learning and growth.

Chapter 4: Martyrdom

Q1. Martyrs are made through suffering and giving up their lives for their beliefs. Of your family and friends, who would you consider possessing a martyr mentality? In what ways do you possess a martyr mentality?

_____
_____
_____
_____

Q2. Sometimes, giving up your life doesn't accomplish the greater good. It just means you have less life. In what ways does this ring true for you?

_____
_____
_____
_____

Q3. Sheepdogs ensure everyone around them is okay and migrating forward before continuing. It's the trap of waiting for the weakest link before you do what is in your heart to do. In what ways have you acted like a sheepdog?

_____
_____
_____
_____

Q4. We become a proxy when we do for others what they will not do for themselves. In what ways have you acted like a proxy?

_____
_____
_____
_____

Q5. Cleaning up someone else's mess because they don't want to do it limits their learning and growth. In what ways have you acted like a cleaner-upper?

_____
_____
_____
_____

Chapter 5

Are You Listening to Yourself?

We've come a long way in understanding why we think the way we do. Neurology has become popular culture, and we are all the better for it. We now understand that the way we talk to ourselves has a direct effect on our mental health. In this chapter, we will identify a few ways that we can get trapped in a negative narrative and what we can do to combat those downward spirals.

Don't Be Helpless. Do Be Empowered.

Martin Seligman is one of my favorite thought leaders. He is often referred to as the father of positive psychology. His book, *Learned Optimism: How to Change Your Mind and Your Life*, was pivotal in teaching me the value of positive thinking and the trap of learned helplessness. Working with so many families in crisis over the years, I have seen my share of helpless behavior, but I couldn't identify what caused it until I read that book.

Seligman defines learned helplessness as, "the giving-up reaction, the quitting response that follows from the belief that whatever you do doesn't matter." He cites a study that has been conducted hundreds of times all over the world, which reveals how learned helplessness occurs. In the study, scientists split animals up into three groups. Group 1 was given control over a lever that could stop an annoying loud noise or shock. Group 2, which he refers to as the helpless group, was in the same environment, hearing the loud noise or feeling the shock, but couldn't push a lever to make it stop. They were reliant on the first group to stop the madness. Group 3 wasn't subjected to noise or shock and didn't have a lever. They were just there. Throughout all of the studies, the results were consistent.

Group 1, the ones who could push the lever to stop the noise or shock, and Group 3, who weren't subjected to it, stayed active and engaged during the experiment, acting like they usually would. Group 2, who could hear the noise or shock but not personally stop it, became lethargic and apathetic. Although they had experienced the same level of negative stimuli as Group 1, they gave up because they couldn't control when it stopped. To drill down even further, when the scientists removed Group 2 from the area and allowed them to control their outcomes, they didn't even attempt to. They just laid there. They had learned to be helpless.

Understanding how helplessness is learned is critical for our well-being and those we care for. Ensuring that our loved ones have agency over their lives and decisions directly offsets depression and the feelings of helplessness. For instance, instead of just telling your kids that you will punish them, you can explain the consequences if they choose not to obey and then let them decide and respond accordingly. This approach teaches our kids that they can choose how to act and experience the outcome of their actions. It works for us too. If you find that you are apathetic and disillusioned, it may be because you feel that what you are doing doesn't matter and that you don't have control over your life. If you want to combat that, identify the areas you control and manage them in a way that empowers you and gives you purpose.

Don't Get Caught in Regret. Do Learn and Move On.

I'm sure there are things that you regret—fooling around with the wrong person, buying something you couldn't afford, saying something you didn't mean, or cutting your own bangs. We've all got regrets. The strange thing about regret is that the ones that haunt us aren't usually focused on what we did, but what we didn't do. We can try to fix our mistakes if we take risks that don't pan out. If we hadn't taken the risk when we needed to, we'd have missed the opportunity of the moment. I call this "should have" regret. We regret the things we don't do more than the things we do.

Some of us are more prone to "should have" regret because we struggle to confront or say what we need to say at the moment. You know, all the times you walked away from a conversation wishing you had said something that you either didn't think of in the moment or couldn't bring yourself to say right then. Why do we ruminate more on what we should have done than what we have done? It is because when we project the decision we wish we had made into the future, we project it with its best possible outcomes.

Let's say we regret not working it out with an old lover. The only reason we are willing to judge our past decision is because we assume that if we had stayed with that person, the relationship would have thrived, and they would be the person we always wanted them to be. If we knew they would be jerks in the future, we wouldn't regret our decision. **"Should have" regret is based on hypothetical future scenarios.** Even if the lover was a jerk while you were with them and turned into a gem later in life, who knows if that would have happened with you still in the mix? Maybe they became a gem of a human because they had to get schooled by someone else.

"Shouldn't have" regret is when we regret what we have said or done. Because we've already done what we regret, we see the real effects of our actions instead of hypothetical ones. We experience the consequences, whether good or bad. This makes it easier to see how the things we regret doing can work toward the greater good. We don't have to imagine what could have been. We see it with our own eyes. This is why some people say they don't have any regrets; if they hadn't experienced it, they wouldn't have learned or been allowed to have what they have now.

Avoid getting caught in the trap of "should have" regret as best you can. It's a complete waste of time and robs your joy for the present and future. You can't go back and change it. You can guess what would have happened, but you don't know what would have happened, so let it go. If there are takeaways from your past, take what you need and leave the rest. You are creating your future right now, so make it count.

Don't Catastrophize. Do Reframe and Look for the Gain.

Catastrophizing is looking at your circumstances through an exaggerated lens and imagining the worst outcome. We catastrophize when we haven't been feeling well for a couple of weeks, but we say that we are always sick. We catastrophize when we accuse our partner of always being late, even when it's only sometimes. We do it when we think our kids are going to miss their only opportunities for success because they didn't do well in their sophomore year. Unfortunately, we catastrophize often, and it's not a healthy way to think.

Looking for the negative or using absolute language isn't only damaging for our mental health; it's a terrible way to treat others. By catastrophizing, we think we are getting the upper hand by making our point. We may see it as a tool to manipulate others to get them to do what we want or to value the things we value.

For some of us, catastrophizing is so ingrained and subconscious that we have no idea when we are doing it. We believe our narrative, even when it's irrational. Have you ever taken inventory of how many times you use all-or-nothing language when talking with others? How many times have you made a bigger deal about something than you should have? How many times have you tried to manipulate others by projecting their behavior in an extreme and negative light? If you are like me, it's a lot, and we need to stop. If you notice yourself doing these things, it's time to reframe.

Reframing is the mental exercise of changing the way you think about something. It involves choosing to see a situation without a negative, limiting, or irrational lens. Reframing invokes hope. A positive outcome in your mind is conjured up in the same way a negative one is, by what you tell yourself about it. When it comes to the future, everything is a presumption. It's not like you know the future, so whatever way you decide to talk to yourself about it, it's still an act of faith. We can quickly reframe by telling ourselves a different story.

I reframe by reminding myself and my kid that a lousy semester in school isn't the only semester in school. I reframe by expecting the best for my and others' futures. I reframe by seeing my gain instead of always looking for the gap in a lofty benchmark I've set for myself.

Reframing is also helpful for changing how we view relationships. In the excellent book *Loving What Is*, Byron

Katie and Stephanie Mitchell offer four valuable questions to help us reframe how we view other people's actions. They are:

1. **Is it true?** Is what I'm saying or feeling definitively accurate?

2. **Can you know that it's true?** If you are accusing someone of thinking or feeling a certain way, how can you know this unless they've told you? If they haven't told you, it's an assumption.

3. **How do you react?** What happens when you believe that thought? Do your thoughts and reactions harm your relationships? Do they cause you worry and stress?

4. **Who or what would you be without the thought?** If you weren't thinking like this, would your situation and relationships be different? Would you be freer?

Another helpful concept in Byron Katie's book is reframing your expectations of other people's roles. I've coined this "expectation tension". **Expectation tension is when we expect someone to act in a way they don't, causing us grief.**

I knew an adult who wanted my husband and me to play a parental role in their lives even though it felt unnatural for us. Although we were pseudo-mentors in their lives, we hadn't raised them in any way. Because they had this expectation of us, they were continually disappointed that we weren't acting like their parents. It was a role that they assumed we would play without our consent. It caused them a lot of heartache and made us not want to be around them because their expectations were unrealistic. If they had just accepted that we were only friends and not their parents, we would have been able to be friends without the unnecessary tension that those expectations were causing.

Expectation tension creeps up all the time when it comes to how people view their biological parents. Sometimes, we want them to be someone they aren't or can't be. We want them to be more nurturing, more helpful, or more honest, which causes us to be mad at them for not living up to our expectations or meeting our needs. We can't make people something they aren't. Change must come on their terms and timeline. We do ourselves and them a disservice when we make internal demands they are unable or unwilling to keep.

We set ourselves free from this needless anxiety and angst when we let them be who they are and reframe our expectations of them to be reflective of who they are instead of who we want them to be. When we think about our own lives, it helps us have empathy. I can only be who I am, and anyone expecting me to be someone else isn't on me. It's on them.

Don't Cloud Your Mind. Do Close Loops.

Brahma Kumaris said, "A task left undone remains undone in two places – at the actual location of the task and inside your head" (Allen). Unfinished things wreak havoc on our minds. The other day, I asked a group of friends what success would feel like to them, and they all said they would feel successful if they had accomplished or completed what they set out to do. We love finishing things, and we hate it when things feel undone. It doesn't matter if it's a conversation that wasn't concluded or waking up to a bunch of dirty dishes. Unfinished things cloud our minds, and a clouded mind bogs us down.

Open mental loops are things we've told ourselves or others that we will do but haven't done yet. They slow us down and drain our energy and confidence. Your mind can only hold so much information at one time. It is continually trying to prioritize unresolved loops. Our brains will keep bringing them to our attention until we close the loop.

Learning how to close loops is a successful strategy at which everyone should strive to excel. Here are a few hacks to declutter your mind:

- When you think of an open loop, write it down on your phone or a notepad with an action plan to gain confidence knowing you are working on it.

- If you lie awake at night thinking of what you must do, write them down quickly to reference them the next day. The act of writing it down allows our mind to rest, knowing that it's not required to keep bringing it to memory.

- Have the conversations you need to have. Bite the bullet and send the email, make the phone call, or text the person you need to talk to. Putting the ball in their court will stop it from bouncing around yours.

- Keep your surroundings as free from chaos as possible. If cluttered or dirty spaces bother you, clean up so you can take on the world. I can't think straight if my house or desk is a mess.

- If you are the type of person who needs to be reminded of the big picture to do what you need to do, take time to remind yourself why you have this open loop in the first place. The reminder of your vision acts as a catalyst to help you complete it.

- Get rid of unnecessary or unrealistic open loops. Sometimes, I open a loop in my mind by adding an unrealistic or untimely goal to my list. For instance, a fleeting thought comes through my mind about something I would love to take on at a later date, so

I add it to the list when I know that I'm not going to try to tackle it anytime soon. When I do this, it creates an open loop that makes me feel unsuccessful when reminded of it. Although I don't know if I'll be able to stop adding those kinds of goals to my list, when I become aware that now is not the time to pursue them or that they are unrealistic, I remove them from my list so they aren't sitting out there as an unclosed loop.

Whether it's making lists, cleaning up, setting appointments, or tackling conversations or tasks, *get your shit done*. Close those loops. Your mind and attention span will thank you.

Don't Detach. Do Connect.

Disconnection is a natural response to pain. When our body and mind don't know how to process hurt, our first response is to disconnect. If someone has upset us, we run away or avoid them. If our body has been injured, adrenaline floods in, trying to keep us functioning in the moment so that we can fight or flee. Disconnection serves a function for our health. However, if we allow the separation to persist, it has devastating results.

For those who have experienced traumatic events, it is critical to process those to stay mentally healthy. The most revelatory book I've read on processing trauma is called *The Body Keeps the Score*. In it, Dr. van der Kolk explains how trauma affects our ability to fully experience life. He describes how trauma causes our self-sensing area of the brain to disengage, reducing its ability to transmit our visceral feelings and emotions because they are causing us pain and terror. In doing so, we lose a sense of self-awareness. He says this of those who have experienced trauma, "in an effort to shut off terrifying sensations, they also deadened their capacity to feel fully alive" (Ch. 6). Our brains have a hard time developing in a connected way if subjected to chronic trauma or childhood trauma during the early stages of development.

Brain scans show that traumatic events cause us to activate the right hemisphere in our brain, which is our visual, emotional, and intuitive side, and deactivate our left hemisphere, where we analyze and use logic. Essentially, we sever our ability to logically process what has happened or is happening to us. This explains why those who have suffered severe trauma often fight chaotic thoughts and can struggle to make decisions.

When I speak with individuals who have suffered physical or sexual abuse, they often describe the sensation as "out of body," as though they experienced it from afar. Treatment for trauma and this disconnectedness of the body and mind is done through reconnection activities. We can reconnect by using words to describe the past and our feelings about it, or through intimacy and friendship with others. We can also reconnect by doing activities that connect our body and mind. Activities like yoga, desired physical touch, exercise, meditation, and play all help bring our body and mind into alignment to be healthy and happy. If you've experienced trauma, seek out opportunities to reconnect through friendship, therapy, and physical activity.

Building Blocks

- Learned helplessness is "the giving-up reaction, the quitting response that follows from the belief that whatever you do doesn't matter." (Martin Seligman)

- Having agency, knowing that you have control over your own life, offsets depression and the feeling of helplessness.

- We ruminate more on "should have" regret than "shouldn't have" regret because we project the decisions we wish we would have made into the future with their best possible outcomes.

- "Should have" regret is a waste of time and robs your joy for the present and future. You can't change the past, so learn and move on.

- Catastrophizing is looking at your circumstances through an exaggerated lens and imagining the worst outcome.

- Reframing is the mental exercise of changing the way you think about something. It involves choosing to see a situation without a negative, limiting, or irrational lens. Reframing invokes hope.

- Expectation tension occurs when we expect someone to act in a way they aren't, causing us grief. We can't change others, so if we want to be happy, we must reframe our expectations.

- I can only be who I am, and anyone expecting me to be someone else isn't on me. It's on them.

- Open mental loops are things we've told ourselves or others that we will do, but haven't done yet.

- To preserve mental clarity, close open mental loops by writing things down, reminding yourself of the larger goal, avoiding committing yourself to unrealistic or untimely things, reducing the clutter around you, and having the conversations you need to have.

- Traumatic events cause us to separate the emotional and intuitive side of our brain from the logical side, which severs our ability to logically process what has happened to us.

- Healing from trauma requires activities that reconnect us with our sense of self. We can reconnect through talking, friendship, therapy, and physical activity.

Chapter 5: Are You Listening to Yourself?

Q1. Learned helplessness is the giving-up reaction or quitting response that occurs when you believe that what you do doesn't matter. In what areas of your life have you learned helplessness?

_____
_____
_____
_____

Q2. If you find that you are apathetic and disillusioned, it may be because you don't feel like you have control over your life. What areas of your life do you feel in control of? How are these areas different from those you feel apathetic or disillusioned about?

_____
_____
_____
_____

Q3. Can you see learned helplessness behaviors in those you care for that you could assist with this concept?

_____
_____
_____
_____

Q4. "Should-have" regret causes us to ruminate on what we should have done. It is particularly toxic because it is based on hypothetical future scenarios. What are some of your biggest "should have" regrets? What do you need to tell yourself to let these regrets go?

_____
_____
_____
_____

Q5. Catastrophizing is looking at your circumstances through an exaggerated lens and imagining the worst outcome. In what ways are you prone to catastrophizing? How can you mitigate your speech and reactions to limit this behavior? Can you pinpoint times when catastrophizing has pushed your loved ones away? How will you remind yourself of this going forward?

_____
_____
_____
_____

Reframing is the mental exercise of changing the way you think about something. It involves seeing a situation without a negative, limiting, or irrational lens. Reframing the way we process other people's actions invokes hope. Four valuable questions to ask yourself from the book *Loving What Is,* by Byron Katie and Stephanie Mitchell, are:

1. **Is it true?** Is what I'm saying or feeling definitively accurate?

2. **Can you know that it's true?** If you are accusing someone of thinking or feeling a certain way, how can you know this unless they've told you? If they haven't told you, it's an assumption.
3. **How do you react?** What happens when you believe that thought? Do your thoughts and reactions harm your relationships? Do they cause you worry and stress?
4. **Who or what would you be without the thought?** Would your situation and relationships differ if you weren't thinking like this? Would you be freer?

Q6. Work through the four reframing questions about a situation you feel particularly hopeless about and need to reframe.

_____
_____
_____
_____

Q7. Expectation tension is when we expect someone to act in a way they aren't, causing us grief. We can't change others, so if we want to be happy, we must reframe our expectations. In what ways are you experiencing expectation tension? How can you reframe the role that person plays in your life so that you can preserve your happiness?

_____
_____
_____
_____

Q8. Open mental loops are things you've told yourself or others that you will do but haven't done yet. They slow us down and drain our energy and confidence. Your brain will keep bringing open loops to your attention until you close the loop. What tactics will you deploy to close mental loops and declutter your mind?

_____
_____
_____
_____

Q9. Trauma and past hurt cause us to disconnect socially and physically. Healing comes through reconnection activities, where we experience control over our bodies and choices. Are there any areas in your life you sense you've disconnected from in mind, body, or spirit? What connection activities can you do that will work toward connectedness?

_____
_____
_____
_____

PART 2
Taking Control

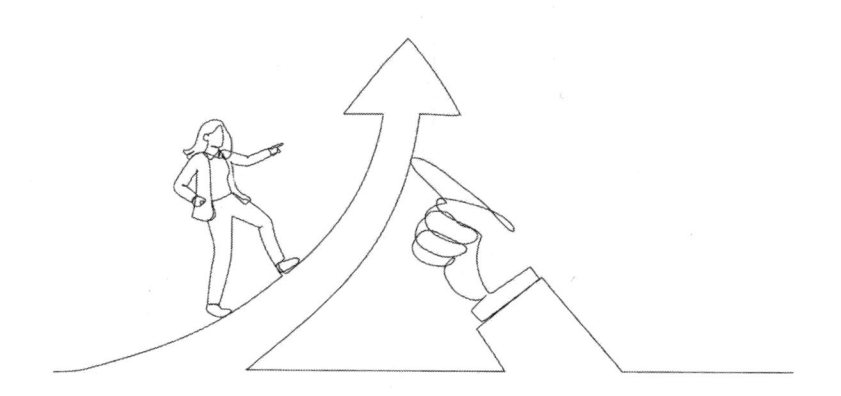

Chapter 6

The Badass You

You Can't Be Someone You're Not

I have an Oscar Wilde quote magnet on my fridge that says, "Be yourself, everybody else is already taken." It's all too easy to fall into the comparison trap. As a young adult, I compared my college experience, relationship status, and job to those of the girls I grew up with. During the first fifteen years of marriage, I would compare my marriage with our friend's marriages. When I was raising children, I would compare myself to other moms. As an insurance agent, I compared my approach and success with other agents. Although comparison is natural and hard to resist, it's a killer.

Apples and Oranges

I have a dear friend I've known since childhood. We have very different personalities, but we were raised similarly, grew up in the same town around the same people, got married, and started having kids in the same years. She's more soft-spoken than me, has a sweet demeanor, and is a quintessential homemaker. When our kids were school-aged, she home-schooled, and mine went to public school. She worked from home, teaching, and I worked outside the home. We both had great kids, but our parenting approaches were different. When something wasn't going well for me, it was hard not to look at my friend's approach and think I must be doing it wrong. Maybe I should be more like her. Then there were times when things weren't going well for her that were okay for me, and I would think, "I must be doing it right." Comparison creates an emotional roller-coaster.

I noticed that once our children were raised and our lives took different paths, all of my comparisons were temporary and faulty. They were temporary because the things I was comparing, like how our kids were doing, changed constantly. Also, parenting comparisons stupidly assume that we know what we are doing and have much more control over our kid's lives than we do. There is no magic formula for good parenting. You just have to understand the uniqueness of each kid. Every kid is different, even if they have the same parents. If you've raised kids to adulthood, you know that our best strategies at the time can turn into regret later, and one strategy may be good for one child but may not apply to another.

One of the greatest comparison traps is to unknowingly compare apples and oranges. In the case of comparing myself with my friend, what I failed to recognize at the time was just how different the lives we wanted were. Because we were in the same stage of life and shared a community, I thought we wanted the same things, even when we didn't. We were working through different playbooks. If you wanted to end up in New York, and I wanted to end up in Las Vegas, comparing the road we took to get there would be silly and unfair.

When I was starting my career as a financial advisor, I worked with some guys who were successful at their jobs. They made a ton of money, rolled with the affluent crowd, and were well-connected. By nature of the competitive environment, it was hard not to compare their annual earnings against my own. They were crushing it, and I was not. After working with them for a while, I came to understand what it took to make the kind of money they were making. Between the twelve-hour days, hob-knobbing, and cut-throat deals, it was apparent that the investment needed to make that kind of money wasn't one I was willing to make. The things I valued, like a flexible schedule and helping my clients invest in low-commission strategies, were never going to help me be successful in that industry. I needed to quit comparing myself to a standard I was unwilling to submit to. If success in that industry held the highest value for me, I would have made the sacrifice, but I valued other things more. I needed to accept the level of financial success my values would yield, and frankly, it wouldn't be as much as the guys I was comparing myself to. We were apples and oranges.

Admire Oprah but Hate Trish?

There's a strange comparison phenomenon. We tend to be happy for people far away doing something we wish we were doing as long as we don't feel like we're competing with them. Jealousy sets in when the same success is proximal to us. For example, I am a fan of Oprah and would love to be able to do the things she does. I don't even try to compare myself to her because we aren't in the same league, so I admire her from afar. But if my friend Trish, who lives in my town or went to school with me, is doing something I want to do, comparison creeps in.

We compare ourselves with those close to us and envy what they do because we see what is possible for someone like us. We should reject the desire to compare and be envious because those emotions are just indications of what we want to do but aren't doing, which is on us. Instead, we should let that proximity inspire us to take the bull by the horns and get what we want out of life. If you compare, make sure you are comparing the same thing. You can't have a Bentley if you want to pay for a Prius.

You Woke Up Like This

In the summer, we live in a little old-mining town called Hope, Alaska. My husband's father left him a cabin there when he died. When we first started dating, we would spend many lazy days hiking and exploring. There was an old, abandoned house by the water that we loved sneaking into. It was dilapidated and falling in on itself. It was kind of the haunted house of the neighborhood and fun to creep around in if you were willing to risk the rotted stairs caving in.

One day, I came across several old Vogue magazines from the 70s. The woman on the cover was curvy and braless, sexy, and voluptuous. I was surprised by the stark contrast of what was sexy in the 70s. Then, in 1993, our idea of sexy was to be waif thin with no boobs. In that moment, I felt this huge sense of relief, understanding that the standard of sexy morphs and changes over time. It was like the angels of heaven gave me the gift of knowing that someday my big boobs and thirty-inch waist might be considered sexy again.

I've fought my body for years, wanting it to be smaller, bigger, or different. Maybe you can relate. It's interesting to see the current trends of huge asses and lips. I often wonder how the body modifications we are making now will play out over time. Will they still be what we want in twenty years? Even if trends stayed the same, which they won't, will butt implants survive the new weight-loss drugs? Will breast augmentation keep my boobs small or perky when I inevitably age or change weight? Probably not, and that's ok.

My point is that we change, what's cool or sexy changes, and our desires change. You are going to keep waking up as yourself, in the body you were born in and with the personality that comes naturally. We can adjust some things, but who we are is fundamental, so instead of fighting it, let's embrace it. Life is hard enough without working against yourself. Love and honor your body, spirit, and personality.

The Power of a Confident Woman

There's not much more powerful than a confident woman. For starters, we are gorgeous creatures who wield a certain type of power. We've got unparalleled intuition and unmatched emotional intelligence. Add all that to our intellect and resilience; we have every reason to be confident. Not to mention that our multi-tasking ability means we have unlimited productivity potential.

When a woman understands her superpowers, she's unstoppable. Do you want to get stuff done? Ask a woman to do it. What's that Christian maxim? When God wanted to save the world, he chose a fourteen-year-old virgin. Confident people are attractive no matter what their gender, but there's something so alluring about a secure woman. Both men and women want to be around confident women. The only ones that don't are those who insecurely want to control us.

Ask for What You Need

I've had employees for more than twenty-five years now, and because of that, I've interviewed a lot of people. In all that time, I've witnessed a consistent variable determining how much people get paid. It's all about what they have the confidence to ask for. It never ceases to amaze me how timid women are when asking for the wage they deserve. Men coming into my office had no problem asking for what they think they are worth. Many have inflated valuations, in my opinion, but women? No, they almost always undervalue their skill sets. The gender wage gap is more complex than women just asking for more money upfront, but it is a major factor. So, ladies, be confident and ask for what you need upfront. Whether it's your pay, what you need from your partner, or negotiating a deal, stating your needs upfront will put you in a better position.

I understand most women have a hard time asking for help. I know I do. Whether you are timid, don't want to seem needy, or are stubborn like me, asking for help is a stretch. The alternative is trying to do everything ourselves, limiting what we can accomplish. I always try to convince myself that I can do it all and look good doing it. It's a fallacy. We do need help sometimes. I've been trying to write this book for a couple of years now, and it kept getting pushed to the back burner. I finally bit the bullet and hired a coach to help me stay on track. Sometimes, we need that extra support.

Willpower isn't very powerful. If you can stop a bad habit or take on a task with sheer willpower, congrats, lean into it. But if you look at your history and see that willpower hasn't worked in that area, you need to adjust and change your tactic. Eliminate bad options so you don't choose them. Surround yourself with people pursuing something similar to what inspires you. Set up external systems and boundaries that keep you on track. Give yourself a come-to-your-senses talk. Honesty is self-protection. If you aren't getting where you want to go, admit it without giving excuses or blaming anyone else. Between your badass self and the resources you have available to you, you are unstoppable.

Move Forward

Perhaps your past or traumatic experiences have limited your growth or confidence. Maybe you are caught up in rehearsing all the ways life has been cruel and unfair. Don't get stuck there.

You can't change the past or other people, but you can process, grieve, and quit letting the people or experiences that hurt you take any more than they already have. Let the past teach you how to move into your future. Have you been in a relationship with a narcissist? Now you know the warning signs and can avoid them. Have you been stolen from? You won't fall for that scam again. A friend betrayed your confidence? You'll be more discerning going forward. Remember, take what you need and leave the rest. You've got more important things to do than drag around a bunch of old baggage.

For the Girls

A couple of years ago, I was feeling pretty low. I think it was one of those inevitable times that happens to mothers whose kids are grown and don't need them as much as they used to. There's a delicate balance of being there for them, while giving them the space to live their lives. Not wanting to be "too much," I started to feel like I should shrink back, somehow make myself less, so that I wouldn't come on too strong. It was getting pretty dark in my mind until I started thinking about my daughters and granddaughters.

I love my daughters and granddaughters and am fiercely protective of them. I want nothing more than for them to live out their fullest, most joyful, and powerful lives. There are things I want to show them and pitfalls I need to warn them about because some life lessons can only come from me, given

I'm the only one who's experienced them. Thankfully, they all have other incredible moms, aunties, and grandmas in their lives, but none of them can play the role I was designed to play. It's important to me that my granddaughters grow up confident and liberated from patriarchal thinking. I need to lean in instead of pull away. Age and the wisdom that comes with it make us more necessary, not less. Your life experience is a treasure for someone; don't shortchange them.

You have women in your life who are looking up to you to show them how to navigate life. Show up and show them, for the girl's sake. Show them how to be a badass. There's a tipping point for all of us when the endeavors we once sought out for ourselves become a part of something bigger, a lesson that can be passed down through the generations. These lessons ground us as people and let us know that we are not alone, but are part of a greater purpose. It's what Indigenous communities have understood and modeled since immemorial: the treasure of elder experience and wisdom.

The story of your life is yours to craft. **The way you interpret your past changes how you remember it. The way you describe your present justifies it. The way you see your future determines it.** Don't let your story be one of victimhood. If our self-talk determines our perception, how much more does our narrative determine other people's perception of us? Your life's story is in your control. Create something great.

Building Blocks

- If you compare, make sure you are comparing the same thing. You can't have a Bentley if you want to pay for a Prius.
- There's a strange comparison phenomenon. We are happy for people who are doing something we wish

we were doing as long as they are removed from us in a way that makes us feel like we aren't competing with them.

- You will keep waking up as yourself, in the body you were born in and with the personality that comes naturally. We can adjust some things, but who we are is fundamental, so instead of fighting it, let's embrace it. Life is hard enough without working against yourself.
- The only people who don't like confident women are the ones who insecurely want to control us.
- Get what you need by asking for what you need.
- Adjust your tactic if willpower hasn't worked. Set external boundaries to help you stay on track.
- Age and the wisdom that comes with it make us more necessary, not less. Your life experience is a treasure for someone; don't shortchange them.

Toolkit

Chapter 6: The Badass You

Q1. We can fall into the trap of comparing ourselves to others who are on a completely different path from us, even though we may be in a similar stage of life or social scene. Identify people you are comparing yourself to. Are you on the same journey, or is it apples and oranges? How is this comparison helping or harming you?

_____
_____
_____
_____

Q2. You are going to keep waking up as yourself; in the body you were born in and with the personality that comes naturally. We can adjust some things, but who we are is fundamental, so instead of fighting it, let's embrace it. Life is hard enough without working against yourself. What practical ways can you love and honor your body, spirit, and personality?

_____
_____
_____
_____

Q3. What are some ways you think you haven't received what you needed because you've failed to ask? How will you remember this life lesson when you get the next opportunity?

_____
_____
_____
_____

Q4. In what areas of your life has willpower not worked? How will you adjust to eliminate bad choices?

_____
_____
_____
_____

Q5. Age and the wisdom that comes with it make us more necessary, not less. Your life experience is a treasure for someone; don't shortchange them. What women in your life should you be sharing your hard-won wisdom with? How will you share it?

_____
_____
_____
_____

Chapter 7

The Decisive You

Some people struggle with indecision more than others. Decision-making is a necessary skill set and can be learned, even if it's more natural for you to take things as they come, being more reactive than proactive. Don't kid yourself; choosing to react instead of purposefully act is still a decision that you've made. Being a good decision-maker is all about optimizing the control you have over your life.

The Catalyst Framework – The Four Ps of Progress

There's a framework I use to help me make decisions and execute with determination. I call it The Four Ps of Progress. Think of a framework as an established guide for thinking about a topic. Academics use frameworks when doing research or evaluating things because they help ensure that the researcher or practitioner considers all the major factors.

I find frameworks helpful because when I'm comparing options, frameworks help keep things in order. They also reduce the likelihood that I will let my excitement about one particular aspect overshadow the other considerations. For example, I was so excited about the possibility of a new job offer that I forgot about all of the elements the new job would affect, nor did I consider if it would be the best option for my family and me. A decision-making framework would help me compare the net salary, the benefits, the commute, upward mobility, coworkers, etc. Having a framework before I consider my options ensures that I don't get all excited about making $4 more an hour, only to lose $6 an hour in benefits.

Making important decisions is hard, and the more emotional we are when making them, the worse off we are. Using decision-making frameworks reduces our emotion-led decision-making. Nobody wants to screw things up, and this fear of screwing up can cause some of us to procrastinate or let others decide for us. We can reduce our fear and potential for errors by using a framework in our decision-making.

The Four Ps of Progress is the framework I developed for my decision-making process. I think about my decision within the context of four main areas:

1. My presence: who I want to be.
2. My prods: what pressures will motivate me to move.
3. My process: the way I get things done.
4. My pace: the timeline for getting to where I need to go.

When I work through each of these Ps, it's easier to come to an action plan, because let's face it, a decision without an execution plan is just another thought.

Presence – Who you want to be.

They say you should always start with the end in mind. I say that you should know who you want to be and start doing what that person would do. It's that old Dolly Parton saying, "Find out who you are and do it on purpose." I think of who I want to be as my presence because that term encompasses how I show up physically, mentally, spiritually, and emotionally. As an exercise, I think about myself ten years from now. I picture how I want to show up in life when I'm sixty. Whenever I hold this mental image, I see myself as an older woman who has aged somewhat naturally, wears fun vintage clothes, is active and strong, has money, collects art, and still works, doing what I love with a schedule that allows lots of time for my kids and grandkids. The individual goals I have for my life aren't highlighted when I look at my future, but I know they contribute to my overall presence. It's hard for me to see the past ten years, so I usually stick with that, but sometimes, I find it helpful to think about my end days and what I want them to be like. We will talk more about what it takes to leave a legacy in Chapter 11, The Legendary You.

Why do I keep this vision of my sixty-year-old self in my mind's eye all the time? Because it helps me make everyday decisions. When I go to buy clothes or get dressed and am tempted to throw something on because it's comfortable or convenient but not at all the style I want to be known for, I leave those sweats on the shelf.

When I say I want to be known for something, I'm not just talking about how other people see or know me but also how I see and know myself. Our presence is all about how we view ourselves. When it comes to your look, if you want to have a certain style, you have to believe it's your style and own it, or else it doesn't work. We've all seen that girl trying to walk in stilettos that don't quite fit and secretly wished for her sake that she would have chosen shoes she could pull off. Your style is one of the ways you express your presence.

I mentioned that I wanted to age somewhat naturally. I'm still very much in decision mode about this. As my hair turns gray and my body sags and wrinkles, I'm having a lot of conversations with myself about what presence I want. Do I want to fight to keep a youthful look, or do I want to make a statement to myself and others that I'm comfortable letting my body take a natural course? Oddly, this becomes a pretty big fork in the road for many of us. Which approach integrates best into who we want to be? It doesn't have to be a major choice, but inevitably, we will have to make decisions around it.

This is what the idea of integrity is all about. All the pieces of you fit into who you want to be, your presence. An easy way to help make decisions is to ask yourself if the action or belief you are contemplating aligns with your values. Will this action or belief change you in the direction of the presence you are envisioning or make it harder to get there? You get the idea.

Every choice we make today sets up our presence in the future. Each one decides how we show up in ten, twenty, or thirty years. The future we want doesn't happen overnight. It's created when we have a picture in mind, draw a line, erase a smudge, paste on a ribbon, and keep crafting our presence.

Prods – What gets you to move.

I've found that people usually fall into one of two categories when it comes to what motivates them: pain or pleasure. In the right circumstances and with enough pressure, either one will get you to move. A prod is a poke designed to get you to move. There's a reason so many behavioral science studies are done on rats in cages pushing levers, and it's because, at a fundamental level, our animal instincts reign supreme. Knowing this, we should utilize motivational tactics that minimize pain and maximize pleasure. Most of us have a preferred prod and you must understand your motivational preferences. Because we are talking about accomplishing goals, which have everything to do with how we see ourselves and want the world to see us, I like to describe pain and pleasure motivators as observable praise or punishment levers.

Praise prods

Many years ago, I ran a marathon. I'm not an avid runner, but I had been jogging for a few months with some girlfriends in the morning. When one of them suggested that we use our morning outings to train for a marathon, I thought it sounded like an awesome goal to hit before I turned thirty. I laced up my shoes nearly every night and ran six to ten miles, usually with my kids accompanying me on their bikes. On the day of the race, I was jazzed. I felt like a total badass. I wouldn't beat any speed records, but if I could finish all 26.2 miles at a decent clip, I would feel like a winner.

There were close to five hundred people at the starting line, and as we began, I started to realize that I hate running in large groups. The thrill of running past someone or getting to the head of the pack is motivating for many, but it had the opposite effect on me. My uncompetitive nature kicked into full swing, and I started intentionally slowing down so that people could pass me. I could over-analyze those actions all day. Was I self-sabotaging? Do I think I'm not worthy of doing well? I don't think it was any of that. What I realized was that I just simply didn't care about my pace as much as I knew the people running next to me did. It was that simple.

For me, it was about completing the marathon, which I did at the pace I wanted. I was working to mark an accomplishment off my list, not to win anything.

I have had moments since then where I have done races because friends wanted to or because I have conned myself into believing that entering and paying for a race registration will motivate me to run regularly. Without exception, this form of motivation has been an epic failure for me. Those races I've signed up for haven't caused me to train or want to run. This type of competition isn't a good motivator for me. Why is this? Because I thrive on competing against my accomplishments, not someone else's. I'm always trying to prove I can do something I've never done before. The bigger the goal, the better. So, once I had done the full marathon, it was checked off my list, and unless I was going to sign up for an ultra-marathon, any accomplishment less than a full marathon didn't hit that praise lever.

People who aren't motivated by competition with others need to identify nuanced and audacious goals that move us in the direction we want to go. Many people love competing against others. For them, the praise lever gets pushed every time they break a record or improve in a specific area. If that's you, harness that prod by looking for opportunities to compete in areas you want to grow.

A praise prod occurs when we feel we can congratulate ourselves or have others congratulate us on accomplishing a goal. Praise prods could be winning an award, making an announcement, getting a promotion, receiving a job well done from someone you respect, fitting into clothes, feeling comfortable in your skin; you name it. It's whatever you would consider a celebration of your accomplishments. If you want to find some motivation, put a praise prod in front of you.

There is a caveat to praise prods. It's best not to celebrate or announce your endeavor until you've met the goal. If you are motivated by praise, announcing your accomplishment or pursuit before its completion will give you the same dopamine bang as if you've already done it, reducing its motivational power.

Are you the type of person who makes lists and loves checking them off because it gives you a sense of accomplishment? Me too. If you are salivating just thinking about crossing things off your to-do list, you are motivated by praise. Remember, praise doesn't have to be from an external source. It can be an internal sense of accomplishment. To harness the power of praise prods, here are some of the tools I've found helpful:

- **Create a dream board:** Create a visual board covered in images and phrases that you want to be part of your identity and keep it somewhere you can see it regularly. I keep mine on my desk. Because it's a dream board, the images and ideals on it are lofty goals; that's the point. I've noticed that since I started doing it, several of the dreams on it have already been accomplished. When that happens, it's time to dream bigger and revise it.

- **Use micro-habits to improve daily:** Micro-habits are small things you can do that work toward an overall goal. For instance, one of the goals on my dream board is to be physically strong, which doesn't happen on its own at my age. So, I've created a list of micro-habits that help me do a little to work toward that goal every day, like twenty-five pushups, squats, lunges, and crunches. You may look at that and think that's not enough strength training to help me get strong, but it is if I do it every day. The point of it being micro is that it only takes me a few minutes to accomplish it. Checking these small goals off my productivity app each day gives me a sense of achievement, and I'm making significant progress over time toward my goal of being strong.

- **Harness the power of affirmations:** Whether it's mantras, meditation, or positive quotes on your fridge or mirror, surround yourself with positivity about your goals. I'm not a touchy-feely person, but my fridge is covered with inspirational quote magnets. They are a constant reminder to me of what is possible. Some people say affirmations to themselves in the mirror. Some listen to a calming mantra on an app. Some people read a self-help book or go to a church service. However you receive your affirmations, it is a positive habit and should be leaned into.

- **Celebrate wins:** Build in your ways to celebrate your accomplishments at each step of the journey. Buy yourself a new dress when you meet your weight goal, go on a trip with your friends when you get a promotion, and make that announcement when you hit thirty days sober. Whatever the win, it should be celebrated.

- **Stay positive:** Let's say that last week, you told me that you were worried about your relationship with your son. It was eating you up inside, and you were having a hard time talking to him about it. The next time I see you, I can tell that you are still concerned, and we have the following conversation:

    - Me: "I remember you wanted to talk with your son about your feelings. How's that going?"

- You: "I'm still worried, but I don't know how to bring it up.".
- Me: "I understand it can be hard initiating that sort of thing. How confident are you that once you start talking with him, it would lead to a deeper conversation about it, like on a scale of one to five?".
- You: "Hmmm, maybe a three?"
- Me: "Why did you choose a three and not a one?"
- You: "Because we've been able to talk in the past, and I'm his mom, so I know him better than anyone."
- Me: "That's great. You're already so close to doing what you feel you need to. I'm sure you'll be able to take that step soon and get this off your chest."
- You: "Ya, I'm going to just do it. He's a good boy, and he knows I love him, so it will be fine."
- Me: "Awesome, I'm excited to hear how it goes. You got this!"

This conversation is an example of how to help people come to an understanding and make decisions about issues they are struggling with. It's a strategy of a behavioral health model called Motivational Interviewing (Motivationalinterviewing.com). It's designed to create conversations that guide and empower people to make meaningful changes on their own terms.

In the example, I asked you to rate your ability to dig deeper during a conversation with your son. There are two ways to process your score of three. I could have asked, "What would it take to get you to a five?" which automatically highlights the gap and the feeling that you aren't where you want to be. Instead I said, "Why are you a three and not a one?" This puts you in a position to recall the strengths in the relationship instead of the weaknesses, highlighting how far you've already come.

This strategy doesn't only work in conversations with others. I question myself this way all the time. If I'm feeling down, I might ask myself how depressed I am on a scale of one to five, and when I give myself a two, it forces me to acknowledge that some things are going right. When you focus on strength, albeit small, it provides enough positivity to make a mental shift that leads to a physical shift. Try it for yourself. You don't have to be a counselor to learn Motivational Interviewing, and it's helpful in all sorts of ways. You can find out more at motivationalinterviewing.com.

Momentum

The point of praise prods is to build momentum. Small wins lead to big wins and greater motivation. When you feel yourself getting better in an area, lean in. Momentum doesn't come every day in every way, so when you have it, take advantage and run with it even if it means you can't give equal focus in other areas. I have a saying that when a door to what you want opens, you better start running as fast as possible and get as far as you can because doors don't stay open forever. It's much easier to keep momentum going than to conjure it up.

We naturally increase motivation when we are good at something. I have a general rule that if I'm naturally bad at a skill like dancing or drawing, I'm only going to work on that skill to the point of needed competency. Meaning, I'll only learn as much as I need to in these areas because no matter how much time I put into learning these skills, they will always be harder for me than for someone naturally good at them.

However, for the areas that come more naturally to me, like public speaking or organizing, I should focus my learning here and harness my natural talent to become excellent in these areas. This approach yields more success, momentum, and expertise in the long run which will drive more investment and joy.

Punishment prods

Pain and punishment can be very powerful motivators. For many of us, punishment is the most powerful prod. When we get uncomfortable enough, we are prompted to change. Motivational gurus like Tony Robbins will tell you that if you want to change, associate enough pain with behavior you don't like, and you will begin to shift.

I chewed my nails as a kid and still struggle to keep my fingers out of my mouth. My mom went to the store and bought that bitter nail polish, so I would experience pain while biting my nails. It was gross, but it wasn't enough of a pain to make me stop. I didn't feel the pain of the bad habit until I was well into adulthood and suffered the embarrassment of trying to present to a client with nails bitten down to the quick. As I was looking down at my hands, I remembered a friend saying how gross it was to see chewed nails. I kept thinking that the client I was talking to probably had the same viewpoint, and the pain of that thought was enough to get me to work on my bad habit.

If you're a competitive person, a good tactic is to set up punishments triggered when you don't meet your goal, like owing a friend money or having to do an undesirable task. For it to be an effective prod, it needs to hurt and be something you dislike.

One of my friends joined a weight-loss gaming site where she bet on her weight loss with a big group of people. They were all given a timeframe to lose a percentage of their weight. If they didn't do it, they lost their money. The bet needed to be enough money to hate the idea of losing it. Those who did meet the goal got to split the pot with the other winners. If you hate losing money but are excited by the chance to win it, gaming may be a good motivational tool for you.

In general, it works to identify what you will lose if you go in the wrong direction. It is supportive to know that if you engage in harmful behaviors, you will lose the people and things you love. A great practice is to imagine how your unwanted behavior plays out over the next year, two years, five years, and longer. Will your continued behavior make your future better or worse? What will you lose if you continue on this path? There are tradeoffs for everything. If you spend all your money on going out to eat now, you will have less to invest in your retirement. If you check out mentally through substances, your ambition and decisions will keep getting kicked down the road, delaying your growth. If you want to change something, identify your pain points and leverage them to make the change.

Process – How you get there.

Do you know the saying, "Life is what you make it"? It's true. Even bad things processed the right way are useful in creating the life you want. Here's another universal truth: you are 100% responsible for your future. Even if you win the lottery tomorrow, if you're a dumb ass with your money, it won't give you a better tomorrow. No one else can build your life. Don't be the woman who just goes along with someone else's plan for your life. It may seem easiest because you don't know what you want for yourself, but I guarantee you it doesn't end well. There comes a day for every woman when they wake up and realize they've been living for everyone else, and there's an overwhelming desire to find themselves. My hope for you is that this day comes sooner rather than later and that you see the necessity of continually working toward your own goals and dreams.

Future thinking – get what you need for what's next

Seneca said, "Luck is what happens when preparation meets opportunity." I couldn't agree more. If there's something you dream about doing or being, no one will make that happen but you. You aren't going to make it happen unless you prepare for it to happen.

When I started my first non-profit benefiting children involved in foster care, I saw how much government policies affected their lives. As a leader in that area, it was natural to get involved in legislative advocacy work. The first time I went to a state capital to lobby for legislation impacting vulnerable families and kids, I had no idea what I was doing. In every meeting with legislators, I kept thinking how much I wished I had paid attention in my high school government class. After a couple of years doing that kind of work, it was obvious to me that if I wanted to elevate my impact, I would need a better understanding of the law.

I decided I wanted to try to get my doctorate in law and public policy. When I said I was going to go back to school, most people didn't understand why I would put myself through that. I didn't need it for my current job. I've never thought like that, though; the type of thinking that tells you to only pursue what is required. Instead, I'm always asking, "What do I need for what's next?"

I had always been a business and finance person, so it was daunting to me to even think about what it would take to get into a program. I got into Northeastern, and my doctoral cohort gathered in Seattle every couple of months. Those first classes were intimidating, to say the least. Most of my cohort had a legal background and a much better understanding of history because they hadn't grown up as sheltered as I was. My ego-saving strategy was to be upfront about how much I didn't know so that my peers would help me instead of mocking me. That strategy worked. They were gracious and kind and taught me a ton. My three-year intensive program taught me more than I could have hoped for. It connected me to professionals across the country, taught me to be a researcher, use better logic, and most importantly, advocate for the families I serve more effectively. It was worth every penny and every late night. I could never do the kind of consulting I do without that education. It's already paid off multiple times.

Over the years, I've mentored entrepreneurs as they've started their businesses or nonprofits. I love planning with them as they work to make their dream a reality. Because the dreaming stage can get disorienting, my counsel on where to start is almost always the same.

1. Identify a handful of people doing what you want to do. Avoid the trap of only looking at the big players. Look at the folks in years one to five who are as close to your area as you can find.

2. Research ideas by talking to people who are successful in the field.

3. Identify the skill sets you will need and start training yourself through school, conferences, videos, and books.

4. Join groups in that field. Show up regularly, get connected, and contribute.

If done right, the vision we start with on any new venture changes as we gather information and put ourselves out there. For many, researching, asking people in the field, and educating themselves becomes the end of the dream because they find out the reality of what they thought they wanted isn't what they wanted at all. The naïve notions of being self-employed so you can be flexible are hit with the reality stick after you talk with enough business owners who have to work much more than when they were employees. Or the idea of making a ton of money starting a restaurant gives you pause when you realize how little profit you would make on every dish.

For some people, this investigative process fuels their dreams. The more they dig, the more inspired they get. The more they learn, the more they want to know. The more they network, the more opportunities arise. Honestly, it can go either way in entrepreneurship, but you won't know until you start arming yourself with the knowledge you need for what's next.

Pace – When you get there.

Bill Gates said, "Most people overestimate what they can do in one year and underestimate what they can do in ten years." We often fail to calculate how long it takes to accomplish something great. We see the end product of someone's work without seeing the years leading up to that success. It's the compounded work over a long period that brings extraordinary results.

One of my sons is a music producer and recording artist. He's been releasing music since 2017 but didn't start making money or have a following until a couple of years later. One of the songs he released toward the beginning of his career became a big hit much later. In fact, I have a gold record hanging on my wall that he presented to us because of that song. According to him, you never know when something will take off. The only thing you have control over is the quality and amount of work product you put into the world. Everything else relies heavily on luck and connections.

I'm the queen of time management, but even my gloriously crafted schedules get thrown off sometimes. My husband and I try to remind ourselves every time we build or remodel a home that it will take two times longer than anticipated and cost us two times more than we wanted to spend. Although we know this from experience, we lose sight of reality too quickly when excited about a project.

Before I start something new or decide to tackle a new goal, I ask myself five crucial questions:

1. **Is this goal something that I have control over?** I don't need to be the only one involved in making it happen, but bad goals are built on other people. They are bad because you can't control other people. Good goals require you to have the ultimate control over whether or not they happen. If I can't make them happen by gathering the right people or doing it myself, it doesn't make the goal list. A bad goal would be, "I have a goal that my son is on the honor roll this semester." A good goal would be, "I will make time each school night to help my son with his homework so that he has a better chance at making the honor roll."

2. **How will I know when I've completed my goal?** Goals need to be measurable, or you won't know if you're progressing and will quit. If you can't define what success means related to the goal, it's not a goal.

3. **Am I able to carry the weight of this goal?** Not every goal is for every season. There is a time for everything, and if it's meant to be, it will keep coming back to you. I've learned that what I can handle has much more to do with the weight I can carry than the time and resources it will take. By weight, I mean the emotional and psychological load of the desire or task. It took me over twenty years to finish my bachelor's degree. I started having kids at twenty-one, about three years into college. For a couple of years, I kept signing up for classes, thinking I could find the time. I hated the idea of not finishing when I was so close. But I was so exhausted raising babies and working, my courses took a backseat every time. I wasted a lot of time and money registering and then withdrawing. I finally realized that I couldn't carry the weight of college in those years. I needed to give myself a break and wait for a time when I could handle it. During those years, I was frustrated with myself because such an important thing in my life wasn't being fulfilled, and I would get discouraged, thinking it would never happen for me. The universe is benevolent, though, and when the time was right, and I knew I could carry the weight, the opportunity came back around.

4. **Do I have the time and financial resources I need to accomplish this goal? If I don't, can I gather the resources I need while working on the goal?** When we want something, it's hard to accept that we may not have what is needed to get the job done. If you want to buy a bigger house but don't have the income to support it, the better goal would be to

build up your income, and once that's done, you can add the goal of buying a bigger house. It's ok to have dreams that you can't make goals yet because you are missing some critical puzzle pieces.

5. **Do I value this goal enough to prioritize it over other things?** It's believed that when we say yes to something, it means saying no to something else. Saying that you value a goal enough to prioritize it over other things means you understand the time and energy it will take to get there, and that time and energy will be unavailable for competing interests. I may have a goal of getting toned arms, but I must not value it that much because I'm unwilling to take time away from my morning reading to make it happen. If a goal doesn't have enough value, it isn't a bonafide goal yet. It's still sitting in the "I wish I would care enough" category, and that's ok. You can't give equal care to everything at the same time.

If the goal I want to accomplish gets a big yes on all five questions, I queue it up and start working on my action plan. If you are like me, you are simultaneously working on several goals. I'm assuming you are because women are notoriously good at multitasking. If you aren't, no worries, just use what is helpful and leave the rest.

Step 1
Write your goal as a measurable outcome with an estimated successful completion date.

Step 2
Underneath the goal, write down every action step that will get you to the goal.

Step 3
Next to each action step, write down who is responsible for that action.

Step 4
Next to the responsible person, write down the estimated completion date/time for that step.

When you are done, it will look something like this:

Goal	Get 30 Amazon reviews of Go Ahead Girl	Completion Date 12/1/24
Action Steps	Responsible Party	Timeline
Email 150 contacts to request reviews	Ted	11/1/24 -11/7/24
Conduct book giveaway on Facebook	Sally	11/7/24-11/17/24
Join 3 author groups and request reviews	Me	11/1/24-11/20/24

As I work through my action plan, I keep adding new action steps that need to be done. Inevitably, I won't know everything it will take when I first start the endeavor, so my lists are dynamic. Each time I cross an item off the list, I feel a sense of accomplishment and know I am one step closer to my goal. Having a list for each goal allows me to manage multiple things simultaneously because I'm only managing the next step of each. This approach keeps me from feeling overwhelmed. A couple of additional action plan hacks:

- ✓ First, tackle any action assigned to you that can be done right now. In doing this, you have started the momentum. The ball is out of your court, and you're now waiting for someone else to do their part. I view it like a pickleball game. The person who wins is the person who scores the most. To score the most, you have to serve the most. So, with every email I write, phone call I make, or new action I take, I am initiating momentum and improving my chances of winning. When I return the serve by responding to a collaborator or adding more action steps, I keep the momentum going.

- ✓ Be reasonable with your timelines and know that they can be fluid. Adjust them as needed. That said, if you have a collaborator in the action plan who isn't completing their tasks promptly, don't let them derail your momentum. Substitute them for a new collaborator or work with them to develop a doable timeframe.

- ✓ If your action steps feel overwhelming, find ways to break them down into smaller steps. For example, if submitting queries to agents feels overwhelming or will take a lot of time, I might break it down into several steps, like drafting a query letter, submitting it to five agents each week, etc.

The ball is in your court. You get to be as decisive and determined as you want to be. Avoid the traps of unhealthy dependency and take little steps every day toward the person you want to be and the goals you want to achieve.

Building Blocks

- Decision-making is a skill set that can be learned.
- Know who you want to be and start doing what that person would do.

- Your presence is who you want to be physically, mentally, spiritually, and emotionally. Picture your ideal presence ten years out and work toward that version of you.

- Ask yourself if the action or belief you are contemplating aligns with your values. Will this action or belief change you in the direction of the presence you envision or make it harder to become that person?

- A prod is a poke designed to get you to move. Prods can be pain, pleasure, praise, or punishment.

- A praise prod occurs when we feel we can congratulate ourselves or have others congratulate us on accomplishing a goal.

- If you are motivated by praise, announcing your accomplishment or pursuit before its completion will give you the same dopamine bang as if you've already done it, reducing its motivational power.

- A punishment prod makes us uncomfortable enough to change.

- If you want to change something, identify your pain points and leverage them to make the change.

- If there's something you dream about doing or being, no one will make that happen, but you, and you can't making it happen unless you prepare for it to happen. Get what you need for what's next.

- It's the compounded work over a long period that brings extraordinary results.

Toolkit

Chapter 7: The Decisive You

The Four Ps of Progress is a decision-making framework that includes the following components:
- Presence – Who you want to be.
- Prods – What gets you to move.
- Process – How you get there.
- Pace – When you get there.

Presence

Q1. Your presence encompasses how you show up physically, mentally, spiritually, and emotionally. What do you want your presence to look like, sound like, and be like ten years from now? What about five years from now?

_____
_____
_____
_____

Q2. Are the ways you are acting, thinking, and carrying yourself getting you closer to the presence you want in ten years or further away? Why?

_____
_____
_____
_____

Q3. What things about your presence could you change that would get you closer to your vision of who you want to be in ten years? Think of two tweaks you could implement today that would get you moving in the right direction.

_____
_____
_____
_____

Prods

A prod is a poke designed to get you to move. There are two ways to do this: pain or pleasure. In the right circumstances and with enough pressure, either will get you to move. I like to describe pain and pleasure motivators as observable praise or punishment levers.

- A praise prod occurs when we feel we can congratulate ourselves or have others congratulate us on accomplishing a goal.
- A punishment prod makes us uncomfortable enough to change.

Q4. How have you used praise prods to get motivated? What does this tell you about yourself? How could you create ways to celebrate your accomplishments?

_____
_____
_____
_____

Q5. How have you used punishment prods to get motivated? What does this tell you about yourself? Can you identify pain points and leverage them to make the change you want?

_____
_____
_____
_____

Process

Q6. When you think about your presence and who you want to be in the future, what skills or knowledge will you need to be that or do that? What steps can you take today to gain that knowledge and start honing those skills?

_____
_____
_____
_____

Q7. If you want to start a new endeavor, how can you gather the information you need using the following tactics?

1. Identify a handful of people doing what you want to do. Avoid the trap of only looking at the big players. Look at the folks in years one to five who are as close to your area as you can find. Who have you identified?

   _____
   _____

2. Research ideas by talking to people who are successful in the field. What did they say?

   _____
   _____

3. Identify the skill sets you will need and start training yourself through school, conferences, videos, and books. What do you need and where will you get it?

   _____
   _____

4. Join groups in that field. Show up regularly, get connected, and contribute. How will you engage?

   _____
   _____

Pace

Q8. Compounded work over a long period is what brings extraordinary results. Think of something you've been successful in. Looking back, think of how that building and compounding occurred. What does this reveal to you?

_____
_____
_____
_____

Five Critical Questions to ask yourself before adopting a new goal:

1. Is this goal something I have control over?
2. How will I know when I've successfully completed my goal?
3. Am I able to carry the weight of this goal?
4. Do I have the time and financial resources to accomplish this goal? If not, can I gather the resources I need while working on it?
5. Do I value this goal enough to prioritize it over other things?

Q9. Think of a goal you've been wanting to tackle. Work through the Five Critical Questions related to that goal.

_____
_____
_____
_____

Q10. Work through your action plan for that goal.

Goal		Completion Date
Action Steps	Responsible Party	Timeline

Chapter 8

The Likable You

One time, I was watching a mayoral candidate debate at a Chamber of Commerce event. There were four candidates in the running, and three of them were men. The female candidate was full of passionate responses and had some ideas that resonated with me, but her presentation was terrible, and it wasn't just one thing. Everything about the way she communicated was rough. Her voice was grating, she kept adjusting her clothes, she wasn't communicating confidently, and her responses were highly charged.

It's not that I preferred the politics of her male contenders, but at least I could stomach their presence for the duration of the forty-five-minute debate. I wanted to like her because she was the only female candidate, but all I kept thinking was, "Why on Earth didn't this woman hire a coach and stylist? She's running for mayor, for god's sake. Surely, she should understand the importance of presentation." But she didn't, and it hurt her chances of being heard.

That's the way it works. You could have the best ideas and be the smartest person in the room, but if no one can stand to listen to you, it doesn't matter much. Although girls typically develop language abilities earlier than boys, we still face an uphill battle when it comes to being heard. According to the American Speech-Language-Hearing Association, our voices are naturally higher, which means they don't resonate as much as lower voices or carry as far, and when we get worked up, we raise them, which makes them even higher (Watson). To add to the frustration, with age, men usually experience greater hearing loss at higher frequencies compared to women. I've been telling my husband for years that our Google Home is a chauvinist pig. I swear it responds to him twice as well as to my commands. It turns out I'm not crazy. Because AI devices like Google Home were originally trained using male voices, they understand them 13% better than women (Label). The research about how unheard and interrupted women are pervasive, but how does that help us? Outside of Google Home being a chauvinist pig and men who do not hear higher frequencies, there are ways to improve our chances of being heard.

Setting the Right Tone

Have you ever been to a diner, and the waitress is an older southern woman who sprinkles "honey" and "sweetheart" into the entire transaction? It's endearing and somehow nurturing because she's older, actually from the south, and it feels authentic. But then, a few weeks later, you are at a diner in Seattle, and the young female waitress tries to do the same. It hits differently, y'all, and not in a good way.

__Be authentic.__ Stay true to your personality and place. I'm all for learning new words so you can improve your vocabulary or adjust your approach when talking to different people, but stay true to your core. I have an older friend who is really sugary sweet in her communication. She'll kill you with kindness. When I first met her, her sugary sweetness really threw me off, and I didn't believe it was her real personality. But after several months of watching her interact with everyone around us, I was proven wrong. She was the real deal, and her loving demeanor continued to both surprise and heal the people who befriended her. Here's the thing though, I could never come across like her. If I added all those niceties to my speech, people would be able to tell I was disingenuous. If you don't mean it, don't say it.

Don't condescend. My grandma Bev was a pastor alongside my grandfather for many years. She was loved by everyone who knew her and had a very interesting approach to evangelizing people for Jesus. Her approach was to befriend people around her and treat them like they were already believers. In doing this, she made people feel like they belonged even before they did. Her approach eliminated the trap of being condescending and treating people like they were different or less than. Politicians, speakers, and changemakers of all sorts use this same approach. Whether you want to lead a movement or make friends, focusing on commonalities instead of differences is a winner every time.

Know your audience. I was selling our house one time, and a realtor friend sent over an associate to take pictures, discuss comparable sales, and get paperwork signed. Unfortunately, the associate didn't come prepared for her audience. She started off assuming we had never sold a home and didn't understand real estate markets, construction norms, or lending. She couldn't have been further off. We had been buying and selling homes longer than she had been alive. It really set me off. After I debunked her strategies because she didn't know what she was talking about, I let her know we wouldn't be using her services and told her kindly that she should have asked a few questions about us before she made her pitch. I said something about it to her because she needed to learn the invaluable "know your audience" lesson if she wanted to be successful in her career. Lord knows I had to learn it the hard way.

When I was a young finance professional managing foundation and corporate funds for organizations, part of my job was to go to board meetings to report on their investments. I learned a couple of hard lessons during those years. The first situation was when I was presenting to an Alaska Native Corporation board. I was communicating in a way I thought was respectful by looking them in the eye, shaking hands, and being assertive. I couldn't figure out why they were not returning my eye contact or responding to my questions in the way I was accustomed to. I went back to the office and told my boss about the strange vibe I was getting. He graciously got me some cultural training before I attended more of those meetings. I learned I was being disrespectful without even knowing it. I looked my elders in the eye and gave advice without being asked first. Classic rookie moves. I try to avoid those mistakes now, but sometimes, I still get schooled when it comes to cultural navigation.

Another time, I had to meet with a large church denomination board. The room was full of white men over seventy. I was in my twenties, a woman, and a new manager for their account. I delivered my presentation assuming they had the same confidence in me that I had in myself. They didn't. To them, I was inexperienced, young, and undeniably female (which was a hard pill to swallow for some of those old guys). Looking back, I should have spent more time upfront building credibility, acknowledging their experience, and approaching the whole situation with a little more humility. Don't get me wrong, sometimes all the preparation in the world doesn't combat egomaniacs, but it probably would have helped them give me a chance if I had approached it differently.

Vulnerability

There's a lot of emphasis on vulnerability these days. When done right, vulnerability is admirable and substantially improves our chances of being liked. When used inappropriately, vulnerability discredits and alienates us. Here are some vulnerability guidelines:

1. You can only be vulnerable about yourself and your experiences. Being vulnerable about someone else is called oversharing or gossiping.
2. Keep private matters private. Social media and public platforms are no place to air dirty laundry unless you need to make a public apology or personal proclamation.
3. When you publicly accuse, shame, or disrespect people, your likability score goes way down. Why? Because if you are willing to do that to someone else, you would be willing to do it to me. This makes you an unsafe person.
4. Oversharing is cringy. Discretion is an art form.
5. As a general rule, celebrate publicly and correct privately.

Teachability

Nobody likes a know-it-all. Being a teachable person is not only a benefit to you but also makes you more likable. If given the opportunity, most people love talking about themselves and teaching others something they know. Why do we like it so much? Because when we share what we've learned, it validates our knowledge and experience. These days, it's not hard to find someone to teach you anything you want to know. The internet and social media are full of instructional videos from various sources. Kids are much more likely to search for an answer on Google than they are to ask their parents or teachers. It's an exciting time to access an instant and free top-notch education.

What online videos and tutorials don't do is connect us personally. We took a blacksmithing class recently, and although we might have been able to learn blacksmithing from a YouTube video, we wouldn't have connected with a local blacksmith and other people interested in the hobby who lived near us. Connections and networking can happen online, but connecting in person is not the same. When you make the decision that you want to learn and grow in an area, finding your people is a tremendous gift.

There's a saying attributed to many, "When the student is ready, the teacher appears." Here's how to be ready for your teachers and improve your relationships with those you want to learn from:

1. Go where the people doing what you want to do gather, online and in person. Opportunity is all about proximity. If you want to be a business executive, join your local Chamber of Commerce, networking groups, and Rotary Club. If you want to be an artist, join the local collectives and attend art events. Commit to participating, and connections will happen naturally. Commitment means more than just testing something out. Dig in and contribute. To be a top performer in any area, you have to be a hard worker, and hard workers don't tolerate those who think everything should come easily and quickly. If you want to earn the respect and trust of the best, commit to working alongside them.

2. Don't ask someone to mentor you. True mentorship occurs organically when a relationship is formed between the mentor and mentee. When you identify someone doing what you want, just start doing what they are doing. To get their results, identify what they are doing that is working and start copying their behaviors. Imitation is the greatest form of flattery. This contradicts the misguided approach of asking someone out of the blue to be your mentor. It's misguided and a turn-off because when you do that, you put the work on them like they are supposed to do something for you instead of you doing the work needed to learn.

3. Ask the right people for advice. I've noticed that the people most eager to give advice are the ones who shouldn't. It should be common sense that taking advice on marriage from a single person is a silly idea. Seeking advice from an unsuccessful entrepreneur is also ridiculous. You've got to love those who don't have kids but are eager to give parenting advice. Look for successful folks and ask them for counsel. They will appreciate being asked, and you will learn from the best.

4. Being teachable means being taught. If you aren't going to take advice, don't ask for it. If you don't want to do the work, don't fool yourself into believing that you can be successful without it. Successful people are learners. They look for ways to gain knowledge and experience. If they see you take their advice and use it to improve, you will have a cheerleader for life, and they will do what they can to make you even more successful.

Building Blocks

- You can improve your chances of being heard.
- Stay true to your personality and place. People can spot a disingenuous person miles away.
- Whether you want to lead a movement or make friends, focusing on commonalities instead of differences is always a winning strategy.
- Always do the work of knowing your audience.
- You can only be vulnerable about yourself and your experiences. Being vulnerable about someone else is called oversharing or gossiping.
- Celebrate publicly and correct privately.
- If you want to earn the respect and trust of the best, commit to working alongside them.
- If you need advice, ask people who are successful in that area.
- Don't ask for advice if you won't take it.
- Learning from and collaborating with successful people will give you your greatest cheerleaders and opportunities.

Chapter 8: The Likable You

Q1. How would you describe your authentic tone?

_____
_____
_____
_____

Q2. Have you ever adopted an unauthentic tone? How, when, and why?

_____
_____
_____
_____

Q3. Think of a situation where you want to gain favor. How can you focus on commonalities and inclusion to reduce the risk of sounding condescending?

_____
_____
_____
_____

Q4. Consider a time when you've misjudged your audience. What did this teach you, and how would you teach this lesson to someone coming up?

_____
_____
_____
_____

Q5. Describe a time when you got vulnerability right. What are your takeaways from that experience?

_____
_____
_____
_____

Q6. Describe a time when you got vulnerability wrong. What are your takeaways from that experience?

_____
_____
_____
_____

Q7. Opportunity relies on proximity to the people thinking the way you need to think. How will you identify them and get closer to those people?

_____
_____
_____
_____

Q8. Who would be a good mentor for you to mimic? How will you observe their behavior?

_____
_____
_____
_____

Q9. Who are the most successful people in the area you want to learn about? How will you ask them for advice?

_____
_____
_____
_____

Chapter 9

The Loveable You

Picking Your Partner

I love that "partner" has become synonymous with significant others or spouses. When I was growing up, we had inferior words to define our romantic relationships, like "my old lady," "baby daddy/mommy," or "other half." I've been married for thirty years now, and I would definitely say that our relationship is more of a partnership.

For fifteen years, my husband Kris and I did a lot of marriage and relationship counseling. We've facilitated many weddings and counseled through a lot of divorces. There was a time when I believed people should try to stay married at almost all costs and that, somehow, staying married put you in a better relationship with God. I don't feel that way anymore. Marriage is just one form of partnership, and who you partner with and for how long doesn't make you more or less right as a person. Even though I don't have the same ideology about marriage today as I did as a pastor, as a happily partnered person, I feel more confident than ever about a few big ideas.

The first idea is that partnerships are compounding. Partnerships are always a product of the partners' character traits. The stronger the trait or personality, the more it influences the outcome. Your love and agreement will continue if you have two strong and loving partners. You will expand on the good things you've built. Although you will struggle, you will go from strength to strength. But, if strong negative traits are present, those compound, too, and the outcomes are usually disastrous.

The cool thing about the effects of compounding is that with the right partner, you will be capable of doing much more than you ever could have alone. Two people pushing in the same direction will always get further than one. Just like how money compounds, you make more by starting with more. The very uncool thing about partnership compounding is that when one partner is constantly in the hole, the other has to work much harder to get anywhere.

So here is my advice: **never pick a weak, distracted, or lazy partner.** There's a reason the good athletes don't pick the worst ones for their dodgeball team, they want to win. Pick a partner as strong or stronger than you in the areas you want to excel in. **The entry fee for a relationship with you should be that they can keep up with you and want to go to the same place you do.** It doesn't mean that you won't experience times of frailty or direction change, but if you are at the point of picking, pick wisely if you want to win. You're choosing someone who will have the power to make your life a whole lot easier or much, much harder. There's no such thing as neutral when you merge with another person.

I've always been a very strong-willed person, and when I was young, I gravitated toward relationships that didn't challenge my will. When my husband and I first started dating right out of high school, he wanted to get married really quickly and asked my dad within weeks of dating me if he could have his blessing to propose. I remember talking with my dad about why I thought he was the "one" for me. It came down to the fact that he was even stronger and more determined than I was, which I hadn't experienced yet, but had the sneaking hunch I would need in the future. Not every person wants or needs someone more willful than them. Sometimes, that makes for a terrible and abusive scenario, but I did, and I knew it. My dad agreed, and we got married three months later. After all this time, I'm still so glad that I identified Kris' strength and determination as the traits I needed most. It meant a lot of power struggles over the years, but it also meant I gained the biggest badass as a life partner. Get real about the top traits you need in your partner and choose accordingly.

Loving Your Partner

I've always hated the phrase "my other half" because it says you are half a person without one. Total hooey. You are a whole person by yourself, and no one else ever needs to make you more whole than you already are. Something significant happens when two people decide to merge their lives: their agreement forms a new entity. It's like mixing blue and yellow paint to create green paint. It becomes impossible to undo the colors' effect on each other. Relationships are like that. All of our baggage, good and bad, gets thrown into the mix. It's just like having a business partner. You are responsible for their losses and reap the benefits of their gains.

I often say that Kris and I built each other into what we wanted in a spouse, which is especially true given how young we got married. I believe the best relationships are created by those who consider themselves artists instead of art.

Art is the finished work you observe.

An artist is constantly working toward a finished work.

Many of us enter into relationships believing we must show up as a finished work of art, our best attributes on display, and our past painted over. This doesn't work because it assumes that we don't change when we change all the time. What you need in a partner now is not the same thing you will need in twenty years. If you stay with the same person long enough, you will have many different relationships within your time together, and you will have to decide if you are willing to recreate yourselves to be what each other needs. This commitment to the creative process as a couple will be the thing that keeps you strong.

When Kris and I were first married, we were firmly committed to marriage and had promised each other that divorce would never be an option for us. Honestly, that's probably the only thing that kept us together in those first couple of years. We liked each other most of the time, but fought all the time. It was miserable. We started having kids a couple of years into our marriage and softened toward each other. Friction has a way of smoothing down rough edges.

The reality was that we really needed each other. We had young kids, owned businesses together, shared finances, and the life we had built depended on the other person showing up. When we got into our first years of being empty nesters, we were in the middle of some major life upheavals, and the things we had always done together either ended or changed. A big shift like being empty nesters is a turn many couples don't make.

I remember the first time we had the conversation that we no longer needed to stay married. I will always remember it as one of the most liberating conversations of my life. I realized for the first time that I no longer needed him. I didn't need him to provide for me, nor help me with the kids. I didn't need him to feel secure or to feel right. Yet, I still wanted him.

We are best friends, and although we don't need each other in the same way anymore, we still want each other. For a reason I can't explain, after twenty-three years of marriage, the ability to choose to stay married was a gift to my soul. Even though we had a happy marriage, the notion that I was supposed to stay married because of my duty to Kris, God, and others was a constraint I hadn't railed against, but was there nonetheless. That choice changed everything for both of us.

Relationships are a journey of creating an art piece together and in each other. What you are looking for in a partner is someone firmly committed to creating beauty with you, in you, and for you. Someone who believes the "bones" of you are worthy of their investment, nurture, and creativity. You need to feel the same about them.

Sometimes, when Kris performed marriage ceremonies, he told the story of an old guitar he loved. It was not the most expensive guitar or the prettiest, but we got it when we were poor, and it'd seen a lot of life. If he went to sell that guitar to someone else, all they would see would be the worn-out frets and scuffed body. It would be worth almost nothing to them. But to Kris, the guitar wasn't beautiful because it was in good shape. It was beautiful because it represented all the songs played on it. Real love does not love someone because they are beautiful. Real love creates beauty. I'm beautiful, loved, protected, and secure now because he helped create those beliefs in me over the years.

My mom made me realize that for your relationship to work, you must believe in your partner's potential for growth and treat them by how you want them to be rather than how they currently are. A perfect example to illustrate this was when I was first married. Kris and I kept fighting about something that stemmed from our immaturity. He wanted me to respect him even though, in my opinion, we hadn't been married long enough for him to really prove to me he was worthy of respect.

My mom offered me great advice that day when she told me to treat him like the man I knew he would become. She believed he would rise to the occasion if I believed in him. It worked. We grew up together, and he became the man I went into the relationship believing he could be.

It takes trust to do this. When you haven't had time to build trust, or rebuild it after it's been destroyed, lending trust can get you further faster than withholding it. After all, aren't you with them because you believe they are the right person for you? Long-term relationships require incredible sacrifice and investment to create the picturesque life you want. You need an artist more than you need a piece of art.

Talk

Designing a wonderful life together involves a lot of creative tension. If you have two artists working on the same canvas, they will come to it with different approaches and pictures of what they want it to look like. It's vital in long-term relationships that we talk to our partners about our visions of what we want our life and family together to look like and things we can and can't live without. Never leave those visions unspoken.

I always found it helpful to walk couples through the process of describing what they wanted in their future relationship. What things were deal breakers for them? It's vital to get those things out on the table so that everyone can fully know each other's expectations. If you can agree on a shared vision, identifying what it will take to become that is the next step. What elements of your picturesque future are the most important? Have you verbally agreed on which things are the most important? If you feel that financial stability is one of the most important elements for a happy life together, does your partner agree to spend in a way that works toward that goal? If you believe that monogamy is essential for happiness, have you discussed exactly what limits and boundaries you want to expect from each other related to other people? Never assume your partner thinks like you.

A friend of mine discovered that her partner had been sexting another gal for months. She was outraged and considered his behavior cheating. He didn't seem to understand her anger. They had never talked about sexting, porn, or non-physical experiences like that. I'm not sure what they ended up deciding was cheating from that point forward, but the experience did get them to start talking about expectations. The more you talk and agree on expectations, the better off you will be.

Show Up

Fairy tales aren't real. There is no such thing as happily ever after. There is, however, such a thing as happier ever after, if you put in the work. Unhappy relationships don't get happier without nurture, and happy relationships don't get even happier without care. In relationships, partners will always believe they give more than others.

We have a running joke in our house that when we see one or both partners in an unhappy relationship start to lose a bunch of weight, dress better, etc., it's usually an indication that they are looking to exit the relationship. Getting themselves ready for the big launch, if you will. We only say this because it's apparent to the majority of everyone from the outside that the people trying so hard now to attract someone new were those who hadn't given that same effort to the partner they already had. There could be several reasons for this, and I'm not negating the reality that unhappiness often manifests itself in hopelessness, but I am pointing out a phenomenon. The hope of something good or better causes people to change.

We can and should put equal or more effort into bettering ourselves for the partner we do have. Imagine if your partner did that for you. Attraction to another person is subjective and unexplainable. We can be attracted to many characteristics in a person that have nothing to do with how they look and everything to do with who they are. We do well when we understand that our partner is attracted to us for the same reason now that they were when we first got together, plus some additions. Hopefully, we've added new facets to our lives that make us even more attracted to each other, like having children together and enduring hard times. We make a mistake when we assume that our partner no longer cares about the things that first attracted them to us and that, somehow, a commitment negates the need to stay attractive.

Our natural attractions don't go away. We still like pretty things even when we are ugly. Just like we want our partners to continue to work on and love themselves, we should be doing the same. Kris calls this "keeping his edge." We have to show up for each other. We have to invest and seek to bring more to the table than we take. If both partners have this mentality, we both win. We want to continually impress each other. This keeps the spark alive. It doesn't matter if it's growing my skills or doing my hair.

I want my partner to feel proud, impressed, and attracted to me until we die. This requires that I show up for myself and for him. I want to show up by being present in my mind and body when we are together, by keeping our sexual spark, and by loving him in the way he receives love instead of just the way I want to give love. Kris and I have very different ways of receiving love. He likes gifts and surprises, but I do not. I want to know the end of a movie before I see it. It's been thirty years, and we still have fights about this sometimes, because no matter how many times I've said that I don't want a gift or a surprise day at the spa, he still has a hard time believing me because he likes those things. Now, if he wants to perform some panty-dropping act, I would much prefer he work around the house or tell me I'm wonderful.

We've had terrible scenarios when we misunderstood how we each needed to be loved. The one time we laughed most about this was when Kris decided to surprise me with a tanning bed in our house. Back then, I went tanning a couple of times a week, and he thought it would be sweet for me not to have to go anywhere to do it. So, he bought a used tanning booth, hauled it up to our study on the third floor, and wired it into the house. He was trying so hard to surprise me with something amazing. I remember that he met me at the front door after work and waited for me to go upstairs and discover it. When I went up to change and saw the huge booth, I rushed downstairs, confused, saying, "Why is there a tanning bed in our study?" That wasn't the reaction he was hoping for.

He had been waiting for me to come home, expecting I would see it, run up, jump on him, and tear his clothes off for the nice gesture. Needless to say, that's not what I did. I wasn't sure I wanted a huge tanning booth in my study. That day was rough. We had been married ten years and still misunderstood what made each other melt. Kris loves it when I tickle his arm. If he tickles mine, I get an emotional rash. When are we going to figure it out? I wish I could say that we have arrived and don't need to have these conversations anymore, but we still do, and that's good because it reminds me to keep thinking of him and what makes him feel loved instead of what is understandable or easiest for me. To be happy, you've got to continue showing up.

Adjust

If we are artists co-creating our lives, we have to be willing to change on a personal level, and as a couple. Navigating life with another person requires adjustments from both parties to keep your life headed in the same direction. Kris and I have often faced our own personal lows. Think of those times as if you are driving a car through a construction zone, and you have to navigate carefully to protect each other and get through it.

There's a certain speed you like to attack life with. I tend to go very fast, and sometimes, my approach to life feels too fast or furious for Kris, my kids, or those who work with me. I wouldn't say that I am haphazard, but I tend to take big risks. It's impossible to be at the same speed as your partner all the time, which is why it's so important to recognize when they are trying to adjust life to offset your speed.

Think of it like this: you are in a car, and the driver is in a big hurry, so they start to drive fast, weaving in and out of traffic. You find yourself stomping on the imaginary break in the passenger seat or yelling at the driver to slow down. You wouldn't feel like you had to do this if they were driving in a way you felt comfortable, but they aren't, and you are nervous. Or maybe you are like me and fancy being a race car driver. You are frustrated when your partner drives slowly, lets other people in, or takes too long to pull out of the parking space. The reactions we see in our partners are as much an indication of their personality as they reveal how comfortable our partner is with our behavior.

I see this play out in so many ways for couples. One partner loves to shop and buy the newest things, so the other partner stresses and nags about their financial situation. Or maybe one partner is the fun parent, so the other feels they have to be the disciplinarian. Perhaps one person switches jobs when bored, so their partner feels like they can't make a change because they are worried their family won't have stability. You get the idea.

These are ways we adjust to each other's behaviors, and sometimes, we don't recognize why we are doing it. We can also blame the other person for the position we find ourselves in while doing what we had to do to calm what we viewed as a tumultuous situation. We don't recognize or talk about why we do what we do enough, so we resort to stewing in our own sauce, making assumptions about why the other person is making their choices. We hate being told no and can feel accused when our partner tries to regulate. We won't change personalities, so understanding why they are regulating can greatly help.

Don't play the blame game. Recognize that your actions really affect your partner, and if you see them adjusting, talk about it and come to a compromise. One of the ways you compromise is by identifying some areas where you can do what you want to do at the rate you want without jeopardizing your life together. This could be hobbies or assigning roles for certain tasks. You also come to compromise when you decide how each of you will adjust what you want and your pace for the intertwined areas of life.

Losing Your Partner

In this chapter, we've only explored how to choose, love, and live happily with the partner you have. But what if you no longer want to stay with your partner? I don't have personal experience in this area because I've been with the same one for most of my life. That said, I, like you, have seen many relationships end. Sometimes, the individuals are better off having ended it—other times, not. What I see more often than

I wish is the repeat of the same relationship pitfalls when those individuals embark on relationships two, three, and four.

So, if you are thinking about ending it, do it with your eyes wide open. Weigh your decision as the smart, capable, reasonable woman that you are. What do you need in a partner? What is the very real cost of staying or going? There are no perfect people, but there are people who better fit together. Don't go looking for a fairytale. You can't fix or save others and can't be happy with someone else until you've decided to be happy with yourself.

Building Blocks

- Partnerships are compounding. They are a product of the partners' character traits. The stronger the trait or personality, the more it influences the outcome.

- Two people pushing in the same direction will always get further than one. But if one partner is unwilling to move or go in another direction, the other has to work much harder to get anywhere.

- The entry fee for a relationship with you should be that they can keep up with you and want to go the same place you do.

- You are a whole person by yourself, and no one else is ever needed to make you more whole than you already are.

- Get real about the top traits you need in your partner, and choose accordingly.

- The best relationships are created by those who consider themselves artists instead of art. Art is the finished work you observe. An artist is constantly working toward a finished work.

- Real love does not love someone because they are beautiful. Real love creates beauty.
- Relationships are a journey of creating an art piece together and in each other. A good partner is firmly committed to creating beauty with you, in you, and for you.
- The more you talk and come to an agreement on expectations, the better off you will be.
- Keep showing up for your partner physically, emotionally, and spiritually. We can and should put effort into bettering ourselves for the partner we have.
- The reactions we see in our partners are as much an indication of their personality as they are a revelation of how comfortable our partner is with our behavior.

Toolkit

Chapter 9: The Loveable You

Q1. What are the key traits you want or need in a partner?

_____
_____
_____
_____

Q2. If you have a partner, what characteristics in one another do you see compounding toward positive outcomes? What characteristics are compounding toward negative outcomes?

_____
_____
_____
_____

Q3. Two people pushing in the same direction will always get further than one. But if one partner is unwilling to move or go in that direction, the other has to work much harder to get anywhere. In what ways are you pulling in the same or opposite directions?

_____
_____
_____
_____

Q4. Describe ways you can approach your relationship as an artist instead of demanding that it be a finished work of art.

_____
_____
_____
_____

Q5. Real love does not love someone because they are beautiful. Real love creates beauty. How can you create beauty with and for your partner? What are some ways they could create beauty in you? How will you communicate this with them?

_____
_____
_____
_____

Q6. What expectations do you have of your partner that you haven't expressed to them? How and when will you discuss those expectations?

_____
_____
_____
_____

Q7. In which ways can you improve how you show up for your partner? In which ways do you wish your partner would show up for you? How will you encourage or discuss this?

_____
_____
_____
_____

Q8. Are there areas of your relationship or situations with your partner when you feel that you have become a "brake" to offset their "gas pedal"? How are you doing this, and why? How will you discuss this with them?

_____
_____
_____
_____

Q9. Are there areas of your relationship or situations with your partner when you feel that your partner has become a "brake" when you are trying to put the "gas pedal" to the floor? Have you misjudged their response? How will you compromise?

_____
_____
_____
_____

Chapter 10

The Empowering You

I was in a work meeting not long ago with a bunch of social service agencies. A counselor used the term "empowering" when describing how they wanted to serve their clients. The meeting facilitator launched into this soapbox speech about how the word "empowering" had a negative connotation because it implied that you had the power to give to someone instead of walking alongside them in their power. Although I understood their comments, which may be a concern when serving vulnerable populations, the facilitator was splitting hairs at best and virtue-signaling at worst. We all know what the counselor meant when they said they wanted to empower the people they work with. They were saying that they wanted to support and encourage their clients and provide strength where needed. Call it whatever politically correct term you want. We could all use more empowering people in our corners.

Power dynamics are at play in every single relationship we have. It's not always the most assertive personality in a relationship with all the power. It may be the one perceived to be the weakest. Tell me, who has more power in a relationship where one person is addicted to drugs and the other person is upending their life to get them clean? It's certainly not the sober partner.

We each hold elements of power in every relationship or organization we are a part of. It can be the person who has the power to make something possible or the person who can make someone do what they want by refusing to do it themselves. When we need things from someone, they have power. When their behavior affects our lives, they have power. When we make decisions that impact us and our families, we have power. Power isn't negative; contrary to popular narratives, it has many positive uses other than oppression. Empowering people give power to others by providing encouragement, resources, or connection.

We each have some level of power and favor within our sphere of influence. We know more than outsiders about our culture and people. Or maybe we've got street smarts or book smarts. It could be that we've just got more experience or been there longer than a newcomer. Everyone has an upper hand sometimes. You know that saying, "It's not what you know but who you know"? The majority of the time, it rings true, and if someone you know is willing to lend you their favor or endorse you, it's a game-changer.

I've been in professional situations where I wasn't empowered, and ones where I was, and the experiences were worlds apart. When I was twenty, I decided I wanted to learn about trading stocks. I was a receptionist at an oil drilling company at the time, and the guys I worked with were always talking about investing. Their conversations were fascinating to me because I'd never been around people who talked about money in that way. Naively, I decided to apply for a job at a major brokerage firm.

I hadn't even graduated college yet, and I knew nothing about finance other than doing some accounts payable work. I got an interview for an administrative job, but I wanted to get into the broker training program. The manager interviewing me laughed when I told him I wanted to be a broker. He then told me that there was no way in hell anyone with real money would give it to a twenty-year-old girl to invest it for them. It was the early nineties and still very much a man's world in that industry. They got away with a lot of garbage back then. Knowing what I know now, he had a point, although he shouldn't have said it. It didn't faze me, though. I figured I would prove him wrong. I got an administrative job and studied for my licensing exams independently. The manager who interviewed me wasn't there for long after I started, and the one who replaced him was much more supportive.

There was an older woman at that firm named Dolly, a broker who encouraged me daily. She worked hard to build a great book of business, and I will always be grateful to her for lending me her influence, knowledge, and power. I eventually became a stockbroker, and at one point in my finance career, I even managed money for governments and foundations. I'm not the best analyst, and I don't possess the ruthlessness that the industry needed at the time, although I did it and was able to experience some success. But honestly, I wouldn't have kept trying without Dolly's empowering spirit during those years. She's still a friend and an encouragement to me.

Years later in my career, I had the opposite experience when I started at a new investment firm. If you're an established broker and switch firms, you're expected to bring your clients with you and get to work. However, I still needed to learn the ropes of the new place and get settled in. I was in my late twenties by then, but I still lacked confidence and was feeling pretty nervous as my new manager was introducing me around the office. There were two female brokers at the office, and neither one had any interest in empowering me in any way. When he introduced me to one, her exact words were, "Good luck," as she smirked and turned back to her screen.

It was a rough start that never got much better at that firm. It turns out that being around empowering people can catapult you to the next level, and being around disempowering people sucks the power right out of you.

I had never been around a super-encourager until I met my husband. I grew up in a community that expected everyone to do right and be right, so no one was given kudos for doing what was expected. Don't get me wrong, I was very supported, but we were too serious about virtue to act like anyone's cheerleader. After all, no one should need a cheerleader, right? I certainly didn't think I needed one until I met Kris.

It was like I was in the Twilight Zone. He told me I was beautiful and amazing a hundred times a day and would brag about me to all of his friends. He had a rough childhood, which taught him that pride and confidence were a strength and protection. I had always been taught that pride came before a fall and should be avoided at all costs. I'd never been around anyone comfortable calling themselves "good-looking" or "strong," but I couldn't help but be drawn to his confidence. It didn't feel arrogant, just settled.

I realized then that being an encourager was like having a superpower. I couldn't deny that everyone wanted to be around him because he made them feel good about themselves. Contrary to my beliefs that you shouldn't puff anyone up, I could see no downside to doing exactly that. Those close to him would get better at things because he kept telling them they could, and he was so willing to share his knowledge and show that he wasn't afraid to try new things. It was attractive. It turns out that everyone is attracted to empowering people, and we all hate haters.

The realist in me doesn't naturally hype people up, but I've worked on it extensively over the years and have become more empowering. My empowerment style is more practical than my husband's, but that's my nature. I want to empower people by offering support, networking, resources, or knowledge, if I have it. This means that I work to connect people and collaborate in ways that make everyone stronger. The most powerful people in life are the ones who understand that the best investments you can make are into the success of another person. Every empowering word and deed has a ripple effect that extends much further than we anticipate. For example, Dolly's encouragement and investment in me led to my finance career. My investment in my teams and friends has contributed to their success, and so on. A kind word and hope go a long way. Just like you could probably conjure up a memory of when someone was mean to you, you probably have memories of someone encouraging you, too.

Elements of Empowerment

Knowing how to empower people requires an understanding of how power works. I find it helpful to think of power as an unlimited resource. Power is energy. It doesn't appear or disappear. It is simply moved from one place to another. You can count on it to be taken, given, shared, and reallocated continually.

Power is negotiated. Each relationship or organization you are a part of has a negotiated power structure. A boss isn't a boss without employees. Both the boss and the employees hold their form of power. A boss can tell an employee to do a task, but that employee decides if they are willing to submit to that mandate. The boss only has the power that the employee gives to them. In this way, power is shared. It would be extremely rare if one person in a relationship held all the power. More commonly, power is a compromise within a context or situation. Maybe one partner is the authority on finances or nutrition, and the other partner is responsible for house management.

When you are feeling disgruntled, take a hard look at the situation and see if you can identify where your power lies and how that arrangement was negotiated. Sometimes, when we feel oppressed, it is because we haven't taken responsibility for the power we already have within the situation. As competent adults, we always have choices. All too often, we default to a disempowered stance because it's easier to place the blame on external forces or people. It's harder to recognize when and how we have given up power and where we need to take responsibility.

All the years I spent volunteering in churches, I struggled with the power structures. Religious organizations are notoriously rife with patriarchal thinking. I could see that women were doing the bulk of the work to keep the organizations running smoothly, but the majority of the decision-making power was in the hands of men. When I felt discouraged, it was easy to blame the age-old misogynistic religious power structures and take on a defeated stance. That is, until I realized that I was one of the people perpetuating misogyny by agreeing to work under it. No one was forcing me to volunteer or serve. I had choices. If I disagreed with the church's stance, I didn't have to involve myself, and could make my opinions known. They would go on without me, but I wouldn't be to blame for it continuing.

We all get some ownership. If your church or denomination is oppressive toward women or marginalized groups, the fastest way to make change is for the people doing the work to stop doing the work and demand change. Nothing would get the attention of male leadership faster than a church without women. Who would teach the kids, make coffee, or pay the bills? Obviously, that's not all that women contribute, but you get the drift.

I had a very insecure employee once who told me that I intimidated her, and that was the reason why she wasn't thriving in the job. It wasn't that there were unrealistic demands or criteria, she said she was just intimidated by me as a woman. Accusing me of being intimidating was her way of blaming me for her insecurity and lack of initiative. What was I supposed to do with that accusation? Change my personality? Maybe I should have become insecure so that she felt better? Hogwash. Intimidation and confidence are both mindsets that we get to choose. When someone pulls that shit on you, see it for what it is and let their accusations slide right off you. No one has time for that garbage.

Power isn't a zero-sum game. Disempowering thoughts stem from the notion that if someone else has power, I have none. This isn't true. Power dynamics aren't a zero-sum game, meaning if one person has power, the other one has none, or if one person gains, the other loses. When I choose to give up power in an area, it does not mean I now have no power. It means that I have chosen to utilize my power in another area.

Who has the power when it comes to politics? The elected official or the donor who contributed to their campaign? The donor understands that they are giving power to the legislator by helping them win, and now the legislator has the power to write and pass laws that affect that donor. You would think that this action puts the legislator in power. However, without the campaign contributions, the legislator wouldn't get into office, so they are now indebted to the donor, giving the donor the power.

The same is true when delegating authority. When I give one of my employees authority or power over parts of my business, it's because I'm negotiating power. This negotiation is a sharing of power that benefits us both. By empowering an employee to take ownership of some of the business, I'm reducing my power over that area, freeing it up to be used in other areas.

When you feel the need to be unnecessarily controlling, or feel insecure in your standing, remind yourself that power is an unlimited resource. You can conjure it up with the right attitude and actions. Giving up some power to others just means that you have more availability to gather that positive energy source from other areas. There are infinite amounts of power at your disposal. You are just a conduit.

The more power flows through you, the more it will flow to you.

Empowerment is an act. It's impossible to empower someone without doing something. Sending good thoughts or vibes isn't empowerment. It's positivity. Empowerment is an act. Tell someone they are doing a good job, give someone more authority, write a letter of recommendation, or speak up when someone is being challenged.

Empowering actions don't have to be all sunshine and rainbows, but they do have to be hopeful. The most obvious and easiest way to empower someone is to encourage them with words or support. When we tell a friend they are amazing artists and show up to their First Friday show, we empower them. We can also empower them when we see them in a slump and remind them that they haven't always felt like this, and things will improve. Sometimes, empowering actions involve challenging behaviors of those we love that don't align with what we know they want for their lives. Having those come-to-your-senses talks where you remind someone of who they are and what their potential is are phenomenal and hopeful ways to empower others.

When you like the makeup on the girl serving you coffee, tell her. When someone's talent amazes you, make a big deal of it. When you appreciate someone, thank them. When you see someone wanting to expand their abilities, give them the opportunity. You can't be an empowering person without action. Make a challenge for yourself and see how many empowering acts you can accomplish each day. I guarantee you that the more empowering you are toward others, the more empowered you will be.

Empowerment Hacks

This section contains four concepts about empowerment that are helpful to keep at the top of your mind as you work to become a more empowering person.

Say it how they will hear it. With the rise of the virtual world and social media, our lives are more public than ever. Some people love this, while others hate it. Virtual public praise and criticism have become staples of our human interaction. Like most of us, I don't mind the vulnerability of social media when things are going well, but I hate it when things aren't going well. Some of us would rather not have people knowing about our private lives, which must be honored if we want to be empowering.

More than once, I've made the mistake of bragging about my kids or friends on social media or to others, only to be asked to stop because it makes the person I'm bragging about uncomfortable. In these situations, I'm reminded that just because I would want my accolades to be bragged on publicly doesn't mean everyone would. I don't have to understand; I just need to honor it. For people that appreciate privacy, empower them privately. After all, it should be about them and not about making you look good. The best rule of thumb is to ask if it's ok to share someone's success before you do it. Another good indicator is to follow their lead. If they aren't sharing, they probably don't want it shared. Empowering acts are only empowering when they are done in a way that is appreciated; otherwise, they have the opposite effect.

If you want to be empowering, don't take disempowering actions. We all get back what we give. Leave public personal criticism and hate to the trolls of society that are too chicken shit to put their names, faces, and resources on the line. Remember that the next time someone leaves you a hateful comment or criticism without addressing it privately. They were too weak and insecure to address it as a strong person and aren't worth your time. Arguing with fools is pointless anyway. No one has ever made an irrational person more rational by arguing with them. It's a mindset they are choosing. Do you want a powerful life? Leave the hate to the trolls that want to live underground. Hold your head up and stay in the light.

Say, "Yes, and…" What do you do if you want to empower someone but see some things in them or their plan that shouldn't be encouraged? Get good at saying "Yes, and…" Encourage the good things by saying yes to those things and adding caveats regarding the gaps that must be addressed. We all know that when someone gives us encouragement followed by a but, we only hear the "but." Listen to the difference between these two statements: "Sharon, I like your new garden planting diagram, but how are you planning to water it?" This comment immediately puts Sharon on the defensive. Or you could say, "Sharon, I like your new garden planting diagram, and I would love to hear about your watering plan." When I add a "but" to a compliment, I've introduced a subtracting word. The "but" acts like a minus sign in an equation and negates my positive response. It also portrays a negative assumption. In this example, I'm implying that Sharon hasn't thought about how to water her garden. Alternatively, suppose I use the "Yes, and…" approach. In that case, my positive sentiments remain intact, and I add more positivity by assuming that Sharon has thought of a watering plan and hasn't told me about it yet. Now, maybe Sharon indeed hasn't thought of a watering plan. My "Yes, and…" brings that up without being a jerk. To be a more empowering person, limit your "buts" and find ways to increase your "Yes, ands…".

Who should carry the weight? There is a limit to what we can carry physically, emotionally, and spiritually. Empowering involves staying cognizant of what others are carrying and lifting their load rather than bogging them down. Sometimes, the most empowering thing we can do is shield our loved ones from information they don't need to carry. It's like gossip. We might want to know something terrible about someone, but does that information usually help us? No, not unless those actions directly affect us, which is rarer than we like to admit. More often, bad news is a toxic weight we carry unnecessarily.

Because of my brutally honest tendencies, this discretion is one I'm continuing to work on. For instance, my kids have told me, "Mom, I didn't need to know that people died on the highway today in a terrible pile-up. It's just depressing, and there isn't anything I can do about it." As embarrassing as it is in the moment of that reality check, I'm grateful because it's teaching me that sharing negative information unnecessarily weighs others down. Before sharing negative information, a good rule of thumb is to ask yourself: 1) does this person need to know this information? and 2) will this information help this person live a freer and happier life? If not, keep your mouth shut. They don't need that weight. Better yet, find something uplifting to share.

Empowerment means keeping agency. We aren't altruistic people. It can be difficult to see when we are helping ourselves by helping others. Me helping my kids clean their rooms before guests came over wasn't because they cared about their room being cleaned, I'm the one who cared. Sometimes, we help others because it benefits us, or we hate watching them struggle. I wish I could say that I haven't seen meals or clothing handed out to people who didn't really want them so that the organization could report to their donors that they served a lot of people. We should continually check our motives and, at the very least, be honest with ourselves and others about them. A lack of transparency undermines empowering actions. We can't help but ask, "What's in it for you?" when someone is helping us. Although it's impossible to remove all intrinsic motivation, remember that the ultimate goal of empowering actions is to lend the tools you have to someone else while they are building their life. Their life, not your life. Empowerment isn't empowering unless it strengthens the life that they want.

Empowering Leadership

If you are an organization or movement leader, there are two very simple strategies for empowering your team.

Communicate vision. The first strategy is to constantly put the inspiring vision of where you are going in front of them. Remind them that they are a part of something extraordinary, something different than the status quo. Create an ethos of being a unit fighting mediocrity and doing something meaningful that solves real-world problems. People feel empowered when they are part of an elite team. Find ways to bring this up every time you are with them. We all want to be part of the solution, part of something bigger than ourselves.

Everyone has a job. The second strategy is to ensure everyone involved has a job and area for which they are responsible. There's nothing more disempowering than wanting to be a part of something but not knowing how you fit in or if you have the authority to act. As a leader, the best way to move people and organizations forward is to ensure every person involved has a job they are responsible for and the resources to accomplish it.

I've built several successful non-profit organizations over the years, which has led me to believe in the power of volunteerism and collaboration. Organizational leaders often make the mistake of hiring employees for every task. When they do this, it removes the need for volunteers and collaborators to step in, almost immediately halting the movement's momentum. Why would someone step up and volunteer when there are paid staff doing the job? People work harder and more passionately when they feel they are sacrificing for a cause they believe in.

I've often said that the greatest poverty we experience as humans is when we feel like we have nothing to contribute or bring to the table. It breeds hopelessness and despair. People need to feel needed. We want to know that if we don't show up, we will be missed and leave a gap. If you want to empower a group, make sure everyone has a task for which they are personally responsible and find ways to continually acknowledge their contribution and how it fits within the greater vision of the group.

Building Blocks

- Power dynamics are at play in every relationship. The strongest personality in a relationship does not always have all the power.
- Empowering people gives power to others by providing encouragement, resources, or connection.
- Being an encourager is like having a superpower. Everyone wants to be around one.

- Every empowering word and deed has a ripple effect that extends much further than we anticipate.
- Power is energy. It doesn't appear or disappear; it is moved from one place to another. You can count on it to be taken, given, shared, and reallocated continually.
- Power is negotiated. The only power others have over us is the power we give them.
- Intimidation and confidence are both mindsets that we get to choose.
- Power isn't a zero-sum game. When you choose to give up power in an area, it does not mean that you now have no power. It means you have chosen to utilize your power in another area.
- The more power flows through you, the more it will flow to you.
- Empowerment is always an action.
- If you want to empower a group, make sure everyone has a task for which they are personally responsible and find ways to continually acknowledge their contribution and how it fits within the group's greater vision.
- To be a more empowering person, limit your "buts" and find ways to increase your "Yes, ands…".
- Before sharing negative information, a good rule of thumb is to ask yourself: 1) does this person need to know this information? and 2) will this information help this person live a freer and happier life? If not, keep your mouth shut; they don't need that weight.

- Although it's impossible to remove all intrinsic motivation, remember that the ultimate goal of empowering actions is to lend the tools you have to someone else while they are building their life. Their life, not your life. Empowerment isn't empowering unless it strengthens the life that they want.

Toolkit

Chapter 10 – The Empowering You

Q1. Power dynamics are at play in every relationship we have. It's not always the strongest personality in a relationship with all the power. Consider a relationship you are in where the balance of power feels misaligned. Who has the power and why? What does this tell you about yourself and the other people involved?

_____
_____
_____
_____

Q2. Empowering people give power to others by providing encouragement, resources, or connection. Who are you actively empowering, and how?

_____
_____
_____
_____

Q3. Power is energy, and it doesn't appear or disappear. It is moved from one place to another. You can count on it to be taken, given, shared, and reallocated continually. It is also negotiated. The only power others have over us is the power we give them. In what areas have you unintentionally given away power, and how did that occur?

_____
_____
_____
_____

Q4. Empowering people limit their "buts" and find ways to increase their "Yes, ands." Think of two instances where you can do this.

_____
_____
_____
_____

Q5. Before sharing negative information, a good rule of thumb is to ask yourself: 1) does this person need to know this information? and 2) will this information help this person live a freer and happier life? In what ways have you weighed people down with negative information they did not need? How will you remind yourself not to do this going forward?

_____
_____
_____
_____

Q6. Bring to mind someone you want to empower. Empowerment is action. What actions will you take to provide encouragement, resources, or connection? How will you ensure that they keep their agency during this?

_____
_____
_____
_____

Chapter 11

The Purposeful You

The Seed in Your Soul

Ryan (not his real name) showed up on our doorstep in the fall of 1996. I was twenty-one years old, and my husband, Kris, was a couple of years older. I remember that I was wearing dark green corduroy overalls because they were the only thing that didn't feel tight against my belly. I was early along in my pregnancy with my first child. I had just gotten off the phone with friends we knew from church who led a downtown youth outreach for at-risk teens. They called to ask if we would consider letting a kid they had just met stay with us for a bit because he was in a bad spot. I didn't know anything about the situation, but they said he was staying just down the street from us and would come over to introduce himself.

The doorbell rang ten minutes later, and I stood face to face with a six-foot sixteen-year-old wearing the baggiest Jango jeans I had ever seen. I'll never forget his smile when I opened the door or the way he clasped his hands in front of himself when telling us that his friends said he might be able to stay with us. We invited him in and sat around our gigantic dining room table, which seated thirteen people and came with the house when we bought it a few weeks prior.

We had just purchased an eight-bedroom house in the middle of a rough neighborhood that had been used as a brothel for the previous twenty-five years. It was called Evil Evelyn's. There was even a sign over the door that we took down when we bought the place. It had been out of commission for a while, but we still had to displace a couple of men and their five-foot-tall stacks of porno magazines when we moved in. We probably used a gallon of holy oil in that place to try to get rid of the bad juju.

As you can imagine, being twenty-one and buying a huge old brothel, we had exhausted our savings on our down payment, so purchasing the furniture needed to fill the house was out of the question. This is how we ended up buying all the existing furniture in the house, like the huge table, all the beds, dressers, and the infamous porn-watching chair. We got all that good stuff for $1,000. Looking back, I shudder to think about the germs we lived in, but at the time, it didn't bother us. We got rid of the gross stuff, like the red velvet chair plopped in front of a TV with pornographic DVDs and magazines. Out of necessity, we kept nearly everything else. We were broke, but we were happy and adventurous.

To get to the backstory, you would have to rewind another year, to when my husband and I were newly married and lived in a mobile home in a safer part of town. We had been driving to this rough neighborhood on weekdays after work to hang out with kids at the Boys and Girls Club and serve them an after-school meal. It was where the kids who didn't go home after school went to eat and be with their friends. A guy named Elgin Jones had started this Kids Kitchen program and recruited us to help him because he knew we were interested in helping kids in that area of town.

One day, during our normal "hang-out" at the clubhouse, we had what I would consider to be a sprout moment. It is one of those moments when you can feel a puncture in your heart that has the potential to take your life in a different direction. The desire to do something significant, but you aren't sure what it is. It's like a little dormant seed in your soul. Then something happens, and you feel it germinate. The little sprout peeks out, and you begin to see what it may become.

For me, this happened on a cold and blustery day. Little snowflakes were falling, but the snow hadn't started to accumulate yet. It was below freezing. The door to the Boys and Girls Club building flew open, and a boy who looked to be about eight or nine was pushing a metal shopping cart over the entryway transition strip. His younger brother was helping him push the cart. It took both of them to get it through the door. They weren't wearing coats. The alarming part of the scene was that their two-year-old sister was sitting in the cart wearing only a shirt, wet diaper, and some sandals. They were freezing.

We got them out of the cart, warmed up, and fed them. The oldest brother told us that they lived down the street and that they came because they were hungry. There was no food in their house. Their mom and her boyfriend had passed out. We drove them home that night when we closed the clubhouse. He had us drop them off two houses away because he knew his mom would be mad if she saw us. It tore my heart out to leave them there, but I had no idea what to do about it. We had seen enough neglect working with those kids to know their story wasn't very different from many of their friends. I felt relieved that they knew where to go for help when things got really bad.

In our warm car, on the way to our warm home in a nicer area of town, we sat there, stopped at the traffic light, silent. We simply didn't know how to process the injustice we saw daily. We had already decided to move into that neighborhood. We felt drawn to the kids we were working with and were willing to buy a potentially depreciating home if it meant we could live where they were.

Weeks before, we had picked up this real estate magazine while walking out of the grocery store. In it was this huge colonial eight-bedroom home with gables and a fantastic long porch and swing. I loved it instantly, and the price was relatively low. So cheap, in fact, that we knew it had to be in a rough neighborhood. Sure enough, it was smack dab in the middle of the area we went to each day. We received solid advice from others that we shouldn't buy the nicest home in a bad neighborhood, so we had already put it out of our minds.

But sitting there in that car, the tentacles of the tree I would become kept pushing their way out of that seed. In my mind, I heard a voice while looking out the window of that car saying, "You are going to go buy that house, and you are going to take in foster kids." It took my breath away. I didn't have the slightest clue about foster care. I didn't know who to call when those kids entered the center earlier that day. I simply didn't understand what I had just heard. I was only twenty-one-years-old. In shock, I looked at Kris, who was staring out the driver's side window. He was quiet. He turned toward me, and I saw tears streaming down his face. This is odd because my husband isn't a big crier and rarely did it back then. I asked him what was wrong, and he just looked at me and said, "I don't know what's going on, but I think we should put an offer on that crazy huge house and take care of kids like those we just dropped off."

We didn't speak for the rest of the ride and barely spoke for the rest of the night. The air was too weighty to breathe.

After a few days, we called a lender and found out we would barely qualify for the loan on that house. So, we made a full-price offer, believing we had heard from God. Then, we heard back from our realtor that our offer had been one of two and that the seller had chosen the other offer. We were so confused and angry at this point. What was that car experience all about? Were we losing our minds? So, for the next couple of months, we kept volunteering at the center, channeled our more rational selves, and started making offers on normal houses in safe neighborhoods. We had misunderstood our calling.

Oddly, every offer we placed on other homes was not accepted. Two months after the day our offer had been rejected, we got a call from our realtor asking if we were still interested in the big colonial-style house on Thompson Avenue. The other deal had fallen through. By then, the seller had fixed everything that came up during the inspection and had lowered the price. We couldn't believe it. The house we felt we were supposed to buy was now less expensive with everything fixed. Maybe we weren't crazy.

So, we bought it and moved into the house, nasty furniture and all. I remember feeling overwhelmed by the filth in the four and a half bathrooms. Our friends didn't help move or clean out the place. What twenty-one-year-old would volunteer for that madness? We were on our own. Let's face it: we were both very young, and I think our friends thought we had lost our minds. We were a spectacle. Something is interesting but terrifying about fanatics like us.

In light of why we bought the house, it made sense that our church friends called us about Ryan a couple of weeks after we moved in. After all, we had the room and heart to do it. We had only been in the house for a few weeks when Ryan rang our doorbell. Sitting at that thirteen-seater table, we talked with Ryan about his current situation. He was from

Canada, and his father had brought him to Alaska a year before, but had since left the town, which is how Ryan had gone into foster care. His mother was deceased, and he had been living a transient lifestyle with his father for most of his life. Although he was in foster care, the Department of Child Services couldn't find a place for him, so they put him in the local teen shelter until a girlfriend said he could stay with her and her mom temporarily. The girlfriend's mom couldn't officially be his foster mom because she was already being investigated for neglecting her biological kids, but it didn't stop Ryan from staying there. The arrangement was not safe, which led Ryan to our front porch.

Hearing Ryan's story made our hearts break. He had no legal documentation of his life, and he wasn't an American citizen, which made getting a job or a driver's license nearly impossible. He was sixteen and stuck. I'll never forget that twenty minutes after meeting him, he asked if we would adopt him. We had no idea how to react. So, we just said, "Let's go get your stuff. We have no idea about what it would take to adopt you, but you can stay with us for as long as you need."

A month after he came to stay, a friend of his in a similar situation who was living at the teen shelter moved in as well. We became his foster parents, and they both lived with us until they were adults and went out on their own. They weren't the only ones. During the four years we lived in that large house, nineteen people lived with us for three months or longer. There were more that stayed for shorter durations. Some were kids in foster care, some were people we met trying to get their lives free from addiction, and some were friends who wanted to live out their beliefs by serving others. Undeniably, it was a fanatical way to live. We were very poor, and it was extremely hard being young adults raising teenagers with lots of past trauma and addictions. Those who didn't think we were insane thought we were martyrs, but neither was true.

I often tell people that they would have done the same thing if put in that situation. If a kid showed up at your door with nowhere safe to go and no one to turn to, most people, if they could, would let them in. We could, and so we did. It was the obvious and right thing for us to do. Looking back, I had no idea that these first sprout moments would turn into the passion on which my life's legacy would be built. The motive of my passion lies not in my general love for children but in my hatred for injustice, and there is no group of people more victimized than children. They are subject to the choices of their parents and every person and system with authority or power over them. They don't have rights as minors. They belong to someone else, regardless of that person's ability or desire to care for them.

Did you know that the United States and Somalia are the only countries in the United Nations Member States that haven't ratified the Convention on the Rights of the Child? The Convention on the Rights of the Child created an international standard of rights for children. These are rights to life and survival, individual identity, protection, freedom from exploitation, education, health care, and justice (United Nations). This international standard of rights was the most ratified treaty of the U.N. in the past twenty-five years, and yet the United States refuses to sign because it would mean that states couldn't sentence children under eighteen to death or life without parole, and it would allow children to have rights that may supersede the rights of their parents if necessary. The United States refusing to stand in solidarity with other nations to say that children have rights makes my blood boil.

My advocacy role has changed significantly over the years. I've founded and run several child welfare nonprofits, written law, published research, and am a child and family policy consultant. My passion has only deepened with time. I believe that this is how life's passion works.

1. It starts with an unexplored emotion that gives birth to action.
2. Your actions turn into a greater sense of purpose.
3. Your purpose infiltrates your identity.
4. Your identity becomes your legacy.

Let Yourself be Disrupted

Have you ever been up late at night and seen a commercial about children starving, and how, for only $30 a month, you could feed and house them? Have you ever felt compelled to keep watching, but turned it off because it was overwhelming? Have you ever heard the story of someone undergoing incredible hardship trying to immigrate, and it made you sick with outrage because you didn't know what to do?

Do you love talking about politics and enjoy political debates?

Are you passionate about environmental issues or health and nutrition?

Do you have overwhelming empathy for those struggling with mental illness or disabilities?

Have you always wanted to volunteer at the food pantry or homeless shelter, but it seemed scary?

Does it sound exciting to coach women through delivering a child?

Do you love to listen to others during their hardships and help them process?

Do you bring home every stray dog or cat you find?

How issues like these confront your spirit indicates where that first seed of your passion is planted. The issues you get most fired up about are the things you *should* be fired up about. We all have our part to play. What makes you react strongly? Lean in there. We are compelled to care about different things, which is humanity's beauty. While we act as a catalyst for change in the areas we care deeply about, someone else enacts change in another area where their passion lies. You don't have to feel like I do about child welfare policy, but I'm sure glad you care about what you care about.

Let's consider our current fight for equality as women. Many women around the world are doing their part to empower all women. Female athletes are breaking records and demanding better wages, elevating women's sports and worldwide demand. In 2022, 8.3 million women were enrolled in undergraduate college compared to 6.1 million men (Nam). Plus, we have higher graduation rates. This is remarkable because we were kept out of higher education for so long. In the U.S., over 12 million businesses are women-owned (United States Census Bureau). We control a large majority of all consumer spending decisions. My point is that these advancements and many others on behalf of women are being fought on different battlefields worldwide. Collectively, we are making change because the people who have a passion for that topic are doing something about it. The world changes with little nudges, not huge leaps.

Do you want to feel purpose? Be a part of something greater in any way you can.

Do You Want to Feel Happy? Give.

Giving is the best anecdote for depression. Anxiety and depression grow when we spend too much time thinking about ourselves. All that naval gazing limits our perspective and causes us to be ungrateful.

It's natural to want to live a stable life without being affected by the tragedy of others. Our bodies and minds are always fighting to maintain stasis, that equilibrium that keeps our lives from feeling too volatile. Maybe you've had so much trauma of your own that engaging someone else's is too much. That would be completely understandable and ok. But we wither up when our lives are only focused on ourselves, which is why it's so important to find an area where you can work for change that doesn't overwhelm you.

For years, I was a foster parent. When I did it, I had the grace and desire to do it. I don't feel that same grace anymore. Now, I work to improve the lives of kids in foster care in a different way, which is no less valuable than when I physically took care of them. There are seasons for everything. Times when we need to go hard, and times we need to let ourselves rest. Life changes, and our capacities change, but what doesn't change is our need and ability to be a person of purpose. Find a way to contribute and get involved in your area of passion. If you can't volunteer, donate. If you can't donate, volunteer. If you can't do either, advocate or spread the word. We all have a part to play. Being a person of purpose will improve your happiness and the happiness of others.

1. Your passion gives birth to action.
2. Your actions turn into a greater sense of purpose.
3. Your purpose infiltrates your identity.
4. Your identity becomes your legacy.

Invest Where it Matters

I believe giving is the sacred secret to a life of joy. When done well, giving is the self-directed redistribution of our affection onto a more glorious endeavor than what lures our hearts inward.

I also believe it is important to view each gift as an investment in people or organizations that are transparent in their finances and true to their mission. I aim to be a knowledgeable and intentional investor.

Giving money never saved anyone. Giving money doesn't add value to the invaluable or give a voice to the voiceless because no such cases exist. **Money simply supplies resources, support, and encouragement to those who already have everything inside them to rise to the occasion they are called to take on.** Our investment is simply an acknowledgment of the strength we see.

Through my philanthropic and consulting work, I've been involved with hundreds of nonprofits. The world is full of amazing, well-intentioned people. That said, not all nonprofits are run well or manage donor funds with fidelity. I encourage you to research any nonprofit you want to be involved with or give at charitynavigator.com.

Building Blocks

- Life's passion works like this: 1) it starts with an unexplored emotion that gives birth to action, 2) your actions turn into a greater sense of purpose, 3) your purpose infiltrates your identity, and 4) your identity becomes your legacy.
- The issues you get most fired up about are the things you *should* be fired up about. How issues like these

confront your spirit indicates where that first seed of your passion is planted.

- Collectively, we are making change because people who are passionate about their topic are doing something about it. The world changes with little nudges, not huge leaps.
- Giving is the best anecdote for depression.
- Find a way to contribute and get involved in your area of passion. If you can't volunteer, donate. If you can't donate, volunteer. If you can't do either, advocate or spread the word. We all have a part to play.

Toolkit

Chapter 11 – The Purposeful You

Q1. The seed in your soul is the spark of passion that births your purpose. It starts with an unexplored emotion that gives birth to action. What issues get you fired up?

_____
_____
_____
_____

Q2. In what ways can you lean into these passions and act?

_____
_____
_____
_____

Q3. Living a life of purpose requires acting on purpose. Connect to people that care about what you care about. What organizations can you be a part of working on the things you care about?

_____
_____
_____
_____

Q4. Giving is the best anecdote for depression. Think of a time when giving helped you gain perspective and improved your outlook.

_____
_____
_____
_____

Q5. What are some ways you can give more?

_____
_____
_____

    Find a way to contribute and get involved in your area of passion. If you can't volunteer, donate. If you can't donate, volunteer. If you can't do either, advocate and spread the word. We all have a part to play.

    Give where it matters. Not all non-profits are created equally. Do some research at www.charitynavigator.org/.

Chapter 12

The Legendary You

I have a mantra I say to myself when I'm confronted with something or someone I don't want to be. "I'm not going down like that."

When I'm aware that I'm not taking care of myself physically, "I'm not going down like that.".

When I am tempted to be hateful or bitter, "I'm not going down like that."

When I see someone cap out in their career because they refuse to learn new things, "I'm not going down like that."

When someone challenges me by saying what I want to do is too hard, "I'm not going down like that."

When I'm tempted to sink into hopelessness, "I'm not going down like that."

This mantra has saved me more times than I can count. It's my reminder that, like any good fighter, I have what it takes to keep getting back up and become what and who I want to be. How you go down in history is completely dictated by how you think and the choices you make today.

For You or To You

There are two fundamental approaches to life. You can believe that the universe, a higher being, or God is orchestrating the world with purpose and that your life fits into that higher purpose. Or you can believe that we are here by happenstance and that our lives simply occur without a larger purpose. Either perspective requires a surrender to the fact that we won't be able to know definitively in this life. Because of this, I choose to believe that our lives are part of a larger plan, and that the universe is benevolent.

I choose this perspective because it feels more empowering than believing everything is happening to me for no reason. When I say the universe is benevolent, I mean that everything happening in my life is happening for me instead of to me. It's happening so that I can learn and grow, which brings me a joyful and fulfilled life. Things are happening for me so that I can give and contribute goodness to other people's lives.

Living our lives with the belief that the universe is benevolent is empowering. This belief will help us move from strength to strength. Even when things are hard, we have everything to gain from this belief and nothing to lose. When a relationship ends, instead of meaningless despair, we say we learned things to strengthen our future relationships. When we get sick, instead of raging at the sky, we tell ourselves that our bodies are fragile, and death is as natural as birth and the destiny of us all. Living in this frame of mind also helps us see other people with an enlightened perspective.

If I believe that the universe is always working for my benefit, everyone and everything is being used for my highest good. It's easy to believe the people you like contribute goodness to your life. It's harder to grasp that even the people you don't like are contributing goodness to your life. Even when they hurt you, they are part of a plan to make you stronger and more resilient for the days ahead. The authors of the *15 Commitments of Conscious Leadership* call other people your allies. They are all part of the purpose to make you great. They are your biggest allies, even if they aren't aware that they are. You have allies everywhere. When you view your friends, acquaintances, and enemies as your allies, you see that everyone is working toward the same goal of making you the strongest, happiest, healthiest person you can be in this life. How awesome is that?

I once read a book called *Never Binge Again*, and the authors posed an interesting tactic for the problem of overeating. They recommend that you imagine you have a little pig in you who is only focused on its satisfaction. The pig doesn't care if it wants what is harmful to you. It just wants to get fed. What the authors are doing is the powerful psychological tactic of creating an enemy outside yourself that you can fight against.

My biggest takeaway from this book wasn't about my diet at all. It had to do with other behaviors I was prone to that had the same ability to take me down if I let them. I went through an internal process of identifying unwanted behaviors or negative thinking I needed to overcome, and I assigned them a "personality" I strongly disliked. For example, there's a lady I used to have to deal with who was inexperienced but felt entitled to respect that she hadn't yet earned. She was a pain in my ass when I had to work with her. After identifying areas in my life where I was feeling entitled, I gave those emotions her face and name, and when I found myself wanting to act like that, I would call her to mind. My reaction to being like her in this way was visceral, motivating me to act differently. I didn't want to associate myself with that kind of behavior or anyone who represented that.

Maybe you are so Zen that you don't dislike anyone, but I doubt it. I wouldn't share your enemy's "personalities" with others, but it is a helpful tool for encouraging yourself to behave differently. We positively use the same tactic all the time. We do it when we say we want to be like someone in whatever area we admire. The tool works in multiple ways. This is just another way to view everyone as your ally.

The End in Mind

Living a life on purpose means that you understand that someday you will die. As a former minister, insurance agent, and financial advisor, I've had a lot of experience meeting with people when a loved one dies. I've identified two major takeaways from these experiences. The first is that taking care of someone's belongings, assets, and debts is extremely stressful for the family and friends of the deceased. This stress strains relationships in an unforeseen way. The saying that death brings out the worst in people is true. The second takeaway is that how the deceased person handled their business before death sends a loud message to those they leave behind. When someone dies with a plan for their family to follow in handling their estate, their loved ones feel cared for and protected. When someone dies without a plan, it can feel mean or neglectful to those dealing with their estate.

Planning for the End

Whether you die poor or rich, planning is still an important act of love that no one should neglect. Here are some general planning guidelines if you want to be a person who exits this life on a good note.

1. Talk to your family and friends about your wishes while you are able. It's so cliché, but you never

know about your next moments, so have those conversations now. Do you want your body to be cremated, buried, or donated to science? Do you want to be kept on life support? Who do you want to make decisions for you if you are mentally or physically unable? Don't assume they will agree; ask them and tell other people who you have chosen to make those decisions. Complete an advanced directive form (easily found online) outlining your medical wishes and give copies to your healthcare providers and family members.

2. Have a will. There is no excuse not to have one. Will templates are easily found online for free or for a small fee. Without one, you leave a mess for your family to clean up and potentially put them in the position of fighting over what they want and think you would have wanted. It gets complicated quickly. Also, when you don't have a will, the courts decide about your property and minor children. A will identifies who your family is, who you want to get custody of your kids, who has the authority to decide things about your estate, and who gets your stuff. When you only have a will, your assets are frozen while they go through a process called probate, where a state court validates your will and designates a person to handle your estate. Probate can take months to years depending on the state and how complicated your estate is.

3. If you have assets like houses, savings or investment accounts, expensive belongings, or any wealth, it is best to have a trust. Think of a trust as the plan for how you want your estate handled. The will gives general instructions, but a trust is more detailed and

describes who and how you want things distributed. The cool thing about trusts is that when you have one, and it legally owns your assets, they can all be distributed as you want without going through the long probate process. When a trust is in place, your loved ones or the trustee get to start making decisions and handling things right away. There are several types of trusts, and they can be as nuanced as you want them. Some types of trusts protect your assets from creditors, lawsuits, and judgments. If you aren't wealthy and have fairly simple family dynamics, you can create your living will inexpensively using estate kits from financial folks online for a small fee. If your situation is more complicated, find a good estate attorney to help you.

4. Review all the beneficiaries on your retirement and life insurance plans anytime you have a life change, like a birth, death, or divorce. Check them every couple of years. Make sure those who get your money are those you want to have it. I've seen ex-spouses inherit everything, leaving the current spouse destitute. I've seen one child inherit everything, leaving their siblings with nothing because they were the only ones born when the beneficiary form was filled out. Believe me, you don't want to go out making those mistakes. They will dramatically affect how your loved ones remember you. Beneficiary forms for retirement plans and life insurance policies trump any other instructions you make in your will or trust. I can't stress it enough, keep those forms up to date.

5. In my hundreds of conversations about life insurance with people, the most common excuse I hear about

why people don't want to buy life insurance is that they don't want to think about losing a loved one or dying themselves. It is as if somehow not thinking about it will avoid the only thing in life that is sure to happen to us all. Here's the reality: you will die, and your family members will die eventually. Having life insurance isn't about you. It's about making sure that your family has what they need to go on living a good life when you do go. Leaving your family the money they need when you go changes their life forever. Don't assume that those you financially care for now will immediately be able to find a job that can support them, especially while grieving. At a minimum, you need to have enough to pay off your debts and provide a ten-year replacement income for anyone who depends on it.

Many years ago, I got into a fight with my cousin, whom I was always very close to. We had been through a lot together, and this fight was a doozie. I said some pretty hateful things that would have completely ended most relationships. A couple of days later, her son died tragically. He was like a nephew to me. I was there for his birth and with him often. I wanted to be there and comfort her, but I didn't know how to do that since we just had a terrible fight. The fight made a tragedy worse than it already was, and I wanted so badly to take back everything I had said. We've since made up and are good friends, but I'm always reminded that I never want that feeling of regret again. Say what you need to say. Forgive. It's a shame that we wait to give eulogies until someone has passed and can't hear how much they were loved and valued. Honor those you love and respect while they are alive.

Above the Fray

I want to live a remarkable life. Since you've gotten this far in the book, I'm sure you do, too. I don't need to be rich or famous, but I want to live a life full of joy and purpose. Women like us want to be proud of who we are. We want the generations after us to be proud of the remarkable women we were. We are women of significance. We do things that matter.

I hope you float through life and see the advantage of being above the fray. High enough to avoid the traps and roots that find their way onto your path. I know there will be struggles and difficulties, but you possess enough grace and resilience to avoid getting bogged down in the madness. I hope you avoid unnecessary chaos by distancing yourself from those who cause it and making smart decisions. Remember, you have the power to take what you need and leave the rest.

I hope that when you look around, you see every experience and person as an ally on your journey to joy, success, and love. Go be the badass woman you were always meant to be.

Building Blocks

- How you go down in history is dictated by how you think and your choices today.
- There are two fundamental approaches to life. You can believe that the universe, a higher being, or God is orchestrating the world with purpose and that your life fits into that higher purpose. Or you can believe that we are here by happenstance and that our lives simply occur without a larger purpose.

- The universe is benevolent. Everything happening in your life is happening for you instead of to you.
- When you view your friends, acquaintances, and even enemies as your allies, you see that everyone is working toward the same end goal: making you the strongest, happiest, and healthiest person you can be in this life.
- Living a life of purpose means that you understand that someday you will die.
- Taking care of belongings, assets, and debts is extremely stressful for the family and friends of the deceased.
- How the deceased person handled their business before death sends a loud message to those they leave behind.

Toolkit

Chapter 12: The Legendary You

Q1. There are two fundamental approaches to life. You can believe that the universe, a higher being, or God is orchestrating the world with purpose and that your life fits into that higher purpose. Or you can believe that we are here by happenstance and that our lives simply occur without a larger purpose. What do you believe, and how does this affect how you live?

_____
_____
_____
_____

Q2. When you view your friends, acquaintances, and enemies as your allies, you see that everyone is working toward the same goal of making you the strongest, happiest, healthiest person you can be in this life. Consider a couple of people that you have viewed as your enemies. How can you reframe your perspective and consider them allies?

_____
_____
_____
_____

Q3. How you go down in history is dictated by how you think and your choices today. What choices can you make today that will determine your legacy?

_____
_____
_____
_____

How a deceased person handled their business before death sends a loud message to those they leave behind. Use the checklist below to help ensure you've taken care of business.

- ✓ **Have a conversation now with your loved ones about your end of life.**
    - o Do you want to be cremated, buried, or donated to science?
    - o Do you want to be kept on life support?
    - o Who do you want to make decisions if you are mentally or physically unable?
    - o Do you want a celebration of life? If so, do you have any requests?
    - o Where will they find your important documents?
- ✓ **Have a will, it identifies:**
    - o Who your family is,
    - o Who you want to get custody of your kids,
    - o Who has the authority to decide things about your estate, and
    - o Who gets your stuff
- ✓ **Get a Trust if you need or want one. They are specific for each person, but generally they:**
    - o Keep your assets out of probate.

- o Define who you want to handle your estate.
- o Define how you want your stuff handled.

✓ **Review and update all beneficiaries on your retirement and life insurance plans.**

✓ **Consider your need for life insurance and get it if you need it.**

✓ **Practice giving living eulogies to those you love. If you want someone to know what they mean to you, say it now while they can still hear.**

Go Ahead, Girl, Join the Community!

Goaheadgirl.org

Toolkits
Go Ahead Girl Groups
Shop
Newsletters
Resources

About the Author

Charity Carmody is a proud fourth-generation Alaskan with a heart as big as the Last Frontier. Alongside her husband, Kris, she's raised four amazing kids and is now the doting grandmother of four lively grandchildren. She and Kris kicked off their adventure as foster parents at just 21, driven by their passion for making a difference in children's lives.

Charity's accolades speak volumes: she's a Champion for Children Awardee from the Alaska Children's Trust, made the Top 40 Under 40 list, and is a celebrated Athena Society Inductee. She's also part of 100+ Women Who Care, because when Charity cares, she goes all in!

Armed with a Doctorate in Law and Policy from Northeastern University, along with a bachelor's in Business and an MBA from Alaska Pacific University (where she's now an adjunct business professor), Charity's got the brains to back up her boldness. Her published research on the Family First Prevention Services Act is just a taste of her academic chops, and she's excited about the release of her debut book, *Go Ahead Girl*.

Starting her career in finance and insurance back in 1994, Charity didn't stop there—she launched her own company, Carmody Insurance Agency, in Anchorage in 2007, proving that when life gives you risk, you manage it like a pro! But Charity's passion doesn't stop at business. She co-founded Beacon Hill, Safe Families for Children Alaska, and the Heart Gallery of Alaska, showing that her dedication to helping others runs deep.

These days, Charity manages her insurance business and is at the helm of the Alaska Impact Alliance as its founder and Executive Director, leading a statewide coalition focused on strengthening families and cutting down on the need for child protective services. And through her company, Beautiful Step Consulting, she's helping others strategize and make their own powerful moves.

References

Allen, David. *Getting Things Done: The Art of Stress-Free Productivity*. New York: Penguin Books, 2015.

Ariely, Daniel and Jeff Kreisler. *Dollars and Sense: How We Misthink Money and How to Spend Smarter*. New York: Harper Collins Publisher, 2017.

Brown, Brene. *Atlas of the Heart: Mapping Meaningful Connection and Language of Human Expereience*. New York: Random House, 2021.

Carnegie, Dale. *How to Win Friends & Influence People*. New York: Gallery Books, 1998.

Dethmer, Jim, Diana Chapman and Kaley Warner Klemp. *The 15 Committments of Conscious Leadership: A new paradigm for sustainable success*. Diana Chapman, 2014.

Duke, Annie. *Thinking in Bets: Making Smarter Decisions When You Don't Have All the Facts*. New York: Portfolio/Penguin, 2018, 2019.

Grant, Adam. *Think Again: The power of knowing what you don't know*. New York, New York: Viking, Penguin Random House, 2021.

Hardie Grant Books. *Pocket Maya Angelou Wosdom: Inspirational Quotes and Wise Words from a Legendary Icon.* London: Hardie Grant Books, 2019.

Katie, Byron and Stephen Mitchell. *Loving What Is.* New York: Harmony Books, 2002.

Label, Orly. *Stanford Social Innovation Review.* 18 October 2022. https://ssir.org/books/excerpts/entry/sounds_like_me#:~:text=Speech%20recognition%20exemplifies%20how%20partial,than%20it%20is%20for%20women. 13 August 2024.

Livingston, Glenn and Yoav Ezer. *Never Binge Again.* CreateSpace Independent Publishing Platform, 2015.

Nam, Jane. *Best Colleges.* 29 April 2024. https://www.bestcolleges.com/research/diversity-in-higher-education-facts-statistics/#:~:text=Diversity%20on%20College%20Campuses,-Diversity%20on%20college&text=Women%20have%20outnumbered%20men%20in,compared%20to%206.1%20million%20men. 14 August 2024.

Nietzsche, Wilhelm. *On the Genealogy of Morality 58681st Edition.* Indianapolis: Hackett Publishing Company, Inc., 1998.

Seligman, Martin. *Learned Optimism: How to Change Your Mind and Your Life.* New York: Random House Inc., 2006.

Sharma, Nidhi, Subho Chakrabarti and Sandeep Grover. "Gender differences in caregiving among family - caregivers of people with mental illnesses." *World Journal of Psychiatry* (2016): 7-17.

United Nations. *United Nations Human Rights.* 20 November 1989. https://www.ohchr.org/en/

instruments-mechanisms/instruments/convention-rights-child. 14 August 2024.

United States Census Bureau. *Census.gov.* 8 February 2024. https://www.census.gov/newsroom/press-releases/2024/nonemployer-business-data.html#:~:text=Highlights%20from%20these%20combined%20statistics,with%20$983.7%20billion%20in%20receipts. 14 August 2024.

Van Der Kolk, Bessel. *The Body Keeps the Score.* New York: Penguin Books, 2014.

Watson, Stephanie. "The Unheard Female Voice." *The ASHA Leader* 2019.

Made in the USA
Columbia, SC
15 November 2024

73f22d50-74e3-4a79-9801-c81ba64f1b1dR01